PUTTENHAM
UNDER
THE HOG'S BACK

PUTTENHAM
UNDER
THE HOG'S BACK

A social study of a Surrey village

by

Ruth Dugmore

with illustrations by
Charles Bone

PHILLIMORE
London and Chichester

1972

Published by

PHILLIMORE & CO. LTD.

Shopwyke Hall, Chichester, Sussex.

SBN 85033 032 7

Text set by Phillimore in 11 pt. Baskerville

Printed in Great Britain by

Redwood Press Limited, Trowbridge, Wiltshire

CONTENTS

ILLUSTRATIONS

ABBREVIATIONS

D.N.B.	*Dictionary of National Biography.*
Gosling	MS. 'Notes on the History of the Parish of Puttenham' in the possession of the Puttenham and Wanborough History Society. (G. B. Gosling was an architect who lived at Kilnfields, Puttenham, a gracious house which he built himself in 1914. He had considerable antiquarian as well as architectural interests and, as a result, he studied the history of Puttenham and left his notes on the subject for the use of future local historians.)
Kerry	Kerry Documents, vols. I-XII. MS. note-books in Derby Public Library. Microfilm copies exist in the library of the Surrey Archaeological Society and in the possession of the Puttenham and Wanborough History Society. (The Rev. Charles Kerry was curate of Puttenham 1868-1874. An assiduous antiquarian, he copied into his note-books extracts from the Church Registers and Churchwardens Accounts (many of which have since disappeared) and he recorded many details of local history from other sources. Having removed to a benefice in Derbyshire, he left all his note-books to Derby Public Library on his death.)
Woods MSS.	(1) The 'Godalming Hundred', consisting of 21 volumes of transcripts of original documents made

by Percy Woods (1897), now in Godalming Library. Vol. 17 includes material relevant to Puttenham.
(2) 'Collections' in 57 volumes, containing much unclassified material, also transcribed from original documents.
(Percy Woods was born in Godalming in 1842. His career as a senior civil servant, first in the Admiralty, and then at the Treasury, began in 1863 and he spent the 20 years of his retirement in writing up the above collections.)

V.C.H. *Victoria County History of England.*

PREFACE

This small book is the story of a village in Surrey from prehistoric times to the present day. I have taken Puttenham as an example of social life during the centuries, but the facts might apply to any village in the county. In the course of writing this I have had invaluable assistance from many sources, some of which have been acknowledged in the footnotes. I would, however, particularly like to thank the following: Mr. Jock Vevers for his great help with the prehistoric period, for reading my MS. and advising me on it; Mr. John Macnab for his encouragement and support of the venture; Mr. Crawford Knox for his information on early Christian times in the district; Mr. Timothy Grimm and Mr. Kenneth Gravett for their help in dating the house in the village; and also, Mrs. Manning, Director of the Farnham Museum Society's Local History Group, Miss Beck, Archivist at the Muniment Room, Guildford and the Rev. S.C. Dedman, Borough Librarian of Godalming for their interest and advice. I am especially indebted to Miss Fenton for her skill in deciphering and typing my MS. and lastly to my husband for his help throughout and particularly for his care in reading my proofs.

I, of course, take full responsibility for any errors that may remain.

Puttenham **Ruth Dugmore**

ADDENDUM

Reference is made on pages 73 and 75 to the 'town well', but when this book went to press its site was not known. However, on Palm Sunday 1972, during matins, one of the four Canadian yew trees, leading to the west door of the church, disappeared into the ground leaving only the tip exposed. Tree surgeons were employed and the tree was brought to the surface revealing a round stone-lined hole, which, judging by the height of the tree, was about 18 feet deep. This is, without doubt, the 'town well'.[1]

1. *Surrey Advertiser*, 7 April 1972.

Prehistoric times

I

FROM PREHISTORIC TIMES TO THE DOMESDAY SURVEY

AN ASCENDING VILLAGE STREET, tree-lined, old tiled roofs rising one above the other to the great church tower, strong and watchful. This is Puttenham under the Hog's Back—an agricultural village for more than 900 years.

Nothing of importance has happened here, almost nothing of national significance, but its history is part of the social life of England and, as such, it has added its mite to the pattern of the centuries. The story of Puttenham begins in the mists of time, when there was no documentary evidence, so that archaeological finds and geological and physical maps must form an essential part of the investigation of the distant past. It is to the maps we must turn first in order to understand the reason for the settlement at Puttenham, since from them we can learn the features of the landscape, the condition of the soil and the changes of climate, all of which help to make up the picture. The archaeological finds help us to plot the route of the invaders, and what emerges is settlement which eventually becomes an agricultural village. It has developed and widened its interests, but it still retains a flavour of the past.

The history of Puttenham differs little from other English villages; nevertheless, like each of them it has its own particular individuality, which distinguishes it through the centuries. Its growth has been slow. During the last 300 years it has barely doubled its population and this only with the help of in-coming residents. Its plan has hardly altered since it first appeared as a 'strung out' village. Its houses extend on both sides of the Street and the church still dominates the whole from the hill on which it stands. Admittedly there is a housing estate, but even that continues the long line of the old village. It has experienced the change from open field farming to the small individual farms of the yeomen in the Tudor Age and has watched these being absorbed into the two or three large farms of today. It has suffered under the Presbyterian rule of the Commonwealth and has wrestled with the great problem of parochial administration in the early 19th century. Its lords of the manor have generally lived their lives apart from the villagers. One or two have been interested in the welfare of the people, but others have merely looked upon their manorial possessions as a means towards financial gain. A long line of rectors, with few exceptions, have lived amongst their people giving help and comfort where it was needed. Sometimes, judging by the Revd. Charles Kerry, they have carried out their duties with a nice admixture of humour and theology.

The story of Puttenham shows no great deeds, no outstanding personalities and no contribution to the nation as a whole. It has been just a quiet village concerned with its own affairs, of great interest to itself, but it has cared little for the wider world, until the two great wars took its young men and changed the parochial tenor of its life. Today, within the Green Belt it is still partly, though not entirely, an agricultural village, as it has been since the first seed corn was sown in the time of Neolithic man. But even before this there is evidence of human presence if not of human occupation.

When the glaciers of the last Ice Age drew back to the North the first inhabitants came to Puttenham using the area as a hunting ground rather than as a place of settlement. But except for this occasional use at the beginning, there is evidence that all the cultures which occupied Southern England during the prehistoric period were also represented in Puttenham at some time. The evidence that they have left in flint, pottery and tumuli shows that the district has found favour with man for at least 10,000 years.

It is probably legitimate to consider Puttenham as a human habitat beginning with the Mesolithic (Middle Stone Age) movement, which started in the south of England about 8000 B.C. At this time Britain was still joined to Europe and subject to a cold north wind that made life austere and the search for new hunting grounds essential. Furthermore, the shelter offered by the southern slopes of the Hog's Back would make Puttenham a suitable centre for the small bands of hunters. There is no certainty that there was a settlement in Puttenham such as

Professor J.D.G. Clark found at Farnham. One may be discovered at some future time, perhaps. The Cutt Mill area is a likely place as encampments were usually placed near running water.

Although Puttenham is only on the extreme edge of the Weald it is very much part of it, since included in its boundaries are two Wealden characteristics—the lower greensand and chalk. The chalk escarpment of the Hog's Back contained the nodules of flint for the implements and the greensand provided warm well-drained soil for the shallow pit shelters used by Mesolithic man. He sowed no crops but lived off the spoil of his hunting—birds, red deer and wild boar would have provided him with his protein, supplemented by the smaller mammals, except the rabbit, that are here today. Evidence of this Mesolithic Age is extensive in Puttenham. The largest tool found is the tranchet axe,[1] a roughly shaped tool with many uses. Numerous examples of skin scrapers, knives and blade implements have been picked up locally.

During the long Mesolithic period the climate became more temperate. New forest trees appeared such as wych, willow and aspen trees and, as the warmth increased the oak, ash, hawthorn and, a little later, the beech and hornbeam began to flourish. By 2500 B.C. the Mesolithic people had died out and a new culture appeared—the Neolithic (New Stone Age). The flints of these men show much more sophisticated techniques. With these they were able to clear the ground of trees more easily, and they began to sow seed corn which gradually led to agricultural settlements and village communities. The change came slowly and the beautiful leaf-shaped and barbed arrow heads of the Neolithic and Bronze Ages found in Puttenham testify to the importance of hunting. Excellent examples of the Mesolithic, Neolithic, and Bronze Age flint artifacts from this area can be seen in the Guildford and Charterhouse Museums.

As the pulse of community life quickened, the roads and trackways developed in importance. The Old Road along the Hog's Back ran from Folkestone to the West Country and trade and movement along it became a vital part of life. A good example of the commerce it might have carried is the porcellanite axe-head from the Tiguebulliagh factory, County Antrim, which was picked up at Britty Hill. A further example of the significance of the Hog's Back trackway is confirmed by two Bronze Age barrows that have been found adjacent to the present road. One of these barrows, recently destroyed during the road developments at the Wanborough cross-roads, was dug by Mr. E.E. Harrison who dated it as belonging to the Wessex culture (1800 B.C.). The second barrow, a short distance along the road towards Farnham was spread on the adjoining field by out-of-work labourers at the rate-payers' expense during the bad winter of 1817.[2] It is thought that this was of the same period as that dug by Mr. Harrison who kindly provided these details.

By 550 B.C. the first of the Iron Age Celtic-speaking people came over from the Rhine. They were a warlike race and they built forts on 'almost every prominent hill in southern England', which 'we may assume ... were the strongholds of small tribal chieftains'.[3] Such a fort was Hillbury on Puttenham Heath. This invasion was followed by a second about 300 B.C. A third wave from Gaul arrived in Surrey in the 1st century B.C. They introduced the 'heavy coulter and mould-board plough' and so 'caused the most important revolution in farming since Neolithic man first grew corn'.[4] These Iron Age people came to colonize and probably merged with the Bronze Age settlers whom they found here.

The Romano-British period was a busy time in the Puttenham district. There seem to have been small farms, or settlements at Lascombe, Hillbury, Jackson's Corner (Starcross) and possibly at the Manor House, and pottery of the period was found by Kerry on Puttenham Heath. A particularly fine cinerary urn containing beads and bones was found in the Manor House grounds; this pot and a very good specimen from Lascombe can be seen in Guildford Museum. It has been suggested that these Romano-British farms 'were within range of the London demand for food supplies'.[5]

In 367 the Picts and Scots invaded Britain. By 410 the Romans had left the country and Vortigern invited the Saxons to come and drive out the Picts and Scots. This they did and they obtained land in Surrey, but a generation later the Saxons drove the Britons westwards and 'ravaged as far as the western ocean'.[6] In 568 and for 20 years afterwards new Saxon settlements appeared in Surrey. Just over a century later, in 685, Caedwalla began his reconquest of Wessex and in 688 he made a gift of 60 hides to Fernham (Farnham) for a monasterium.[7] From now on the Saxons began to seek settlements. The Saxon thegn with his followers had to get food, both for themselves and for their ox-teams. Consequently he would choose land which could most easily and most quickly be worked.[8] Almost certainly he found what he needed on the medium loams of Puttenham. The very name supports this view as names ending in 'ham' (home) indicate early Saxon settlements. Hence when we come to Domesday we find a Saxon Thegn, Tovi, in possession of Redessolham (Rodsall), now a farm in Puttenham. The origin of the name Puttenham is uncertain. It may be derived from a Saxon thegn called Putta who possessed a homestead—ham—there. The name appears elsewhere—Putney, Puttenden, a manor near Limpsfield, Puttenham in Hertfordshire and the first bishop of Hereford was called Putta. It is possible, therefore, that a group of Saxons arrived in Britain from the Continent and scattered. Another theory is that the name came from the large chalk pit which lies in Puttenham just south of the Hog's Back—'Put' meaning pit. Whatever the derivation, the word certainly indicates Saxon settlement. Having settled here, they began a systematic clearing of the forest lands.

Probably the village, as such, is of late origin, but settlement of the area is very early, partly because of its fertile soil and partly because of its accessibility from the oldest trackway in England—the Old Way. This accessibility was increased by the network of paths through, or surrounding, Puttenham. The Hog's Back was open in winter and summer for trade East and West. There were three parallel trackways here—on the chalk at the top, a little lower down just above the water line and along the base of the hill. It is not surprising that Puttenham, Seale and Compton, grew up along this route. Another trackway can be traced from Shalford to Farnham passing Hillbury, the Iron Age fort on Puttenham Common. This trackway is one of the many that seem to indicate that the settlement, which was later to be known as Puttenham, was the centre of ancient roads and paths and, perhaps developed as a result of this fact. F.H. Hughes in his paper *The Countryside of Godalming,* speaks of an early road which ran from Godalming, perhaps from the Punchbowl, through Thursley and Elstead, past Hillbury Camp to Tongham.[9] He also notes that there are 46 footpaths and bridle ways from the Portsmouth Road, Hurtmore and Priorsfield Road running up to the Hog's Back. Many of these are of early origin and would have passed through Puttenham, thereby preventing the isolation of a settlement there.

These Saxon villages–Seale, Puttenham and Compton situated on the southern slopes of the Old Way came very near to disaster at the time of the Norman invasion. In 1066 two sections of the Norman host proceeded towards Winchester 'laying waste on their way the manors of Wanborough and Farnham amongst others'.[10] 'The Evidence of the Domesday stands to show the magnitude of the sufferings ... of places near the route of the plundering horde'.[11] We have no evidence to show that Puttenham suffered unduly at the hands of the Normans and 20 years later we find that Redessolham (Rodsall) was held by a Saxon thegn, Tovi.

These few pages, in which the story of the invasions and settlements of Puttenham are told, span over 8,000 years starting back in the mists of time. On reading them it might seem that the invaders came hot-foot on each other's heels; this was not so for hundreds, and even thousands, of years separated them. Each wave as it advanced came a step nearer to permanent settlement in an agricultural village and the inhabitants were thankful for the fertile soil which has offered a living to the villagers of Puttenham until the present day.

The earliest historical document we have of the county of Surrey is the Domesday Survey. It is so competent a document that its compilation without modern clerical aids seems almost incredible. It tells a great deal about individual places, but there is always some obscurity which appears impenetrable. Professor H.C. Darby, however, has shown us how to extract the maximum information from its terse descriptions and from him we can learn something about the county as a whole and of the villages in particular. He points out that Domesday Surrey appears thinly populated and probably unimportant. The thick woodland and heavy clay made cultivation in many places extremely difficult, although other parts on the lower greensand were more productive. Some villages which appear years later are not mentioned, but occasionally a farm is noted; he cites several of these, of which Rodsall is one. The name Puttenham does not appear until 1199, but the manor of Rodsall (Redessolham), a farm in the village today, is given in Domesday. The same applies to Ash which is noted as Wyke, later a part of Ash. He shows too that soil conditions are important for understanding Domesday. In the South West of Surrey, in the Wey valley, the lower greensand is productive and it is along this that Professor Darby notes the existence of several Domesday villages.[12] These, he says, have similar physical features which are mentioned in the Survey, including meadow land and wood. Rodsall or Redessolham, is one of the places mentioned although named, not as a village, but as a manor. This entry of Redessolham is comparable to the pattern of other Surrey villages appearing in Domesday and it gives some view of the manor in 1086, even if a somewhat vague one. It states:

Terra Epi Baiocencis
in Godalming Hd.

> The Bishop (of Baieux) holds in demesne Redessolham. Tovi held it in the time of King Edward and could go with it where he pleased. It was then taxed for 5 hides; now it is not taxed. The plough land consists of two carucates and two acres of meadow. There are three villeins and four cottars. The wood renders four swine. In the time of King Edward and afterward and now it is worth 40s..

The bishop annexed Redessolham to the Firm (Manor) of Bronlei (Bramley).

What does this terse description tell us of Redessolham? First the name—this is probably derived from the Anglo Saxon 'sol' which means a wallowing place for deer, deer 'at wallow' and Redes may indicate the red soil in this part of the village. Sol also appears in the name Soland (Shoelands today). The bishop is Odo of Bayeux, a kinsman of William the Conqueror, to whom William had given 25 manors, several of which were in Surrey, including Bramley and Rodsall. Who Tovi was we do not know. He was obviously a Saxon thegn and the phrase 'he could go with it where he pleased' probably means he could put it under the protection of what lord he pleased.[13] As Odo already held Bramley he naturally included Redessolham in the 'Manor of Bronlei' as part of the demesne.

The agricultural conditions which appear in the survey of Redessolham are similar to those in many of the Surrey entries and they comply with the standard items mentioned by Professor Darby—hides, plough lands, plough teams, population and value.[14] We find that the manor consisted of 5 hides. A hide was originally a portion of land which could normally be cultivated in a year by a full plough team of eight oxen, on an average of about

120 acres. So we can assume that the manor of Redessolham consisted of about 600 acres. This acreage, however, is only conjectural as, by the time of Domesday, a hide had become a unit of assessment without any fixed relationship to the amount of land represented by the term; hence the statement 'it was *taxed* for 5 hides', but it is probable that 600 acres was about the size of the manor. When we come to plough lands the entry is more specific. These 'consist of two carucates'. A carucate was reckoned at about 120 acres—the amount which could be tilled by eight oxen in a year. This would indicate that there might have been 240 acres under the plough and 16 oxen on the manor. Thus the hides, plough lands and plough teams mentioned in the Survey of Redessolham follow the standard pattern noted by Professor Darby in the Surrey entries in Domesday. The agricultural workers are given as three villeins and four cottars. If these are multiplied by five to include families the population would be about 35 and added to these were the servants of the demesne, so it is probable that the number of inhabitants was about 50. Lastly the value of the manor is entered as 40s., but 'it is not taxed'. These statements of the population and value of Redessolham satisfy Professor Darby's fourth and fifth points of similarity, but the addition of the words 'it is not taxed' suggests that Redessolham rendered service in some other way than by taxation. From the fact that the manor lies on the route from London to Winchester, it can be conjectured that when the King was on progress between these two places he would stop at Redessolham and 'live off it', probably leaving it almost bankrupt. The reference to meadow—about two acres—is in agreement with Professor Darby's view that settlements in the Wey valley all seem to have possessed meadow land, a very valuable asset as it provided grazing for the stock. Lastly, the statement that 'the wood yields four swine' substantiates Professor Darby's statement that these same villages all had some woodland. Pigs were very necessary animals in this early economy, as they formed almost the only means of meat protein available to the villagers. The wood, therefore, was valuable for feeding the pigs on beech mast and for this right of pannage the agricultural workers had to 'render' to the lord four swine. This number could indicate that there were about 32 pigs on the manor but the Surrey folios do not show the ratio between the number 'rendered' and the total number of swine.[15] No

church is mentioned although it does not follow that there was none, as Professor Darby considers that the Domesday entries of churches does not cover all those which existed at that time.

We can now visualize this manor of Redessolham as being of about 600 acres lying in the fertile valley of the Wey with a population of, roughly, 50 men, women and children, 16 oxen on the manor, eight belonging to the villeins and cottars and, perhaps, 32 pigs. The last statement in the Survey tells us that it was annexed to Bramley by Bishop Odo and so it remained as part of the manor of Bramley until the 16th century.

This description may not give a very clear idea of Redessolham in 1086 and there is no mention of Puttenham, in fact there is no mention of it anywhere until 1199, over a hundred years later. Nevertheless, it seems permissible to read 'Puttenham' for 'Redessolham' and to imagine the little cruck houses of the villeins and cottars of the manor situated in the village street and the three common fields, which they worked, stretching south west to Redessolham and north to the Hog's Back.

NOTES

1. Surrey Archaeological Collections, vol.xlvi, p.107.
2. Kerry, vol.iii, p.41.
3. Elfrida Manning, *Saxon Farnham*, Phillimore, 1970, p.2.
4. Ibid., p.4.
5. Ibid., p.8.
6. Ibid., p.11.
7. Ibid., p.16.
8. Ibid., p.21.
9. F.H. Hughes, *The Countryside of Godalming and District and its natural features*, 'Growth of a Town', No.4 (Lecture given at the County Branch Library, Godalming 1968), Godalming 1969, p.17.
10. F.J.C. Hearnshaw, *The Place of Surrey in the History of England*, 1936, p.55.
11. Ibid., p.54.
12. *The Domesday Geography of South-East England*, edited by H.C. Darby and Eila M.J. Campbell, C.U.P. 1962, p.404.
13. *V.C.H. Surrey*, vol. i, pp.301-302.
14. Op. cit., p.371.
15. Op. cit., p.386.

II

THE MANOR OF PUTTENHAM IN THE THIRTEENTH CENTURY

EVIDENCE OF THE EXISTENCE of Puttenham is late. The first time the name is mentioned is in a document of 1199, stating that Geoffrey de Bocanton exchanged lands in Puttenham for lands in Stoke.[1] The earliest extant indication of a settlement is the Norman pillars in the Church, which date from c.1160. This architectural evidence suggests that there must have been a village large enough to warrant a church by the middle of the 12th century. However, the name 'Puttenham' is of Saxon origin; thus it can be assumed that there was an earlier settlement and, in all probability, that this lay along the trade route on the greensand south of the Old Way. This type of village strung out along the road exists today and has certainly not been altered, but simply extended.

As we have seen, Redessolham, the modern Rodsall, is mentioned in Domesday as a Saxon manor under Tovi and, at the time of Domesday, probably possessed a population of about 50 persons. There is no evidence as to where these villeins and cottars had their dwellings, but when the position of the three fields of the manor is discussed there may be a case for suggesting that they lived along the present Street and that Tovi's Saxon gehurs and colsetles (the Domesday villeins and cottars) were the first to settle there. In 1086 Odo of Bayeux included Rodsall in his manor of Bramley and, when documentary testimony appears, Puttenham is part of the manor of Bramley. It looks, therefore, as if the village had grown out of the manor of Rodsall. The first lord of the manor of Bramley who is mentioned in connection with Puttenham is Ralph de Fay, who in 1203 granted some land in 'Puteham' to Robert de Barevill. Thus, by the beginning of the 13th century, we can imagine that Puttenham had an identity of its own though as part of the manor of Bramley.

The events in Puttenham at this time are very obscure and so is the picture of the village. We get occasional glimpses into the past from such documents as there are but, even if they are tantalizingly few, they are helpful. In 1199 we find that Gilbert de Barevill was ordered to choose 12 knights who were to regain a virgate of land (about 30 acres) which was held by Roberto de Barevill in the royal manor of 'Puteham'.[2] In the same year Ricardu le Curt rented one virgate in 'Puteham from Thurberti de bosco'.[3] Thus by 1199 the existence of a royal manor of Puttenham is established. By 1203 we are able to gain a little more information. 'Rodolphus de Faia' gave land at 'Solands' to 'Roberto de Barevill' for the rent of a golden spur.[4] 'Solands' is the old name for Shoelands, at the west end of the village. The geographical description of this land given in the document just referred to is complicated, but it is stated that it ran from the ditch to the house of Turberti des Bosches and a vineyard is mentioned as another boundary. The ditch may mean the moat, which is marked on the Ordnance Survey map and which probably surrounded the original house of Shoelands. The mention of a vineyard is interesting. There were a number in Southern England in the early Middle Ages, but certainly not on all manors. However, Puttenham, on the south slope of the Hog's Back, must have been warm enough to justify the growing of vines; this would be another crop to be gathered in by the manorial villeins. We have no knowledge of Turberti des Bosches, but he must have had a house on the road from Seale to Puttenham; it may have been in a wood, judging from his name 'des Bosches'. The document is not dated, but it is probably the one referred to in the Gosling MS. dated 1203.[5]

For nearly 20 years Robert de Barevill must have been in possession of this land, because in 1221 we find that he received from the King ten oaks for the mending and rebuilding of his houses in Puttenham.[6] This document would seem to refer to the existence of a number of houses in Puttenham and by the gift of ten oaks from the King it looks as if de Barevill held his land 'of the King' and not 'of de Fay'. The houses which de Barevill wished to rebuild would have been those of his agricultural workers. The oaks would be used to erect the small cruck houses which were the dwellings of the villeins and cottars in the early 13th century. After this date there is no mention of the de Barevill family. In

1235 there was an alienation of land at Shoelands to Selborne Priory, which may have been part of the de Barevill possessions.

In 1245 the first monastic influence appears, since Peter de Ryvall gave to the convent of Selborne a carucate of land at 'Shulands'.[7] This is quite a considerable gift, because a carucate is about 120 acres. There is no indication as to where this land was situated, but it must have been near the old moated house of Shoelands, which lay a little south-west of the house existing today. Peter de Ryvall was a kinsman, probably an illegitimate son, of Peter des Roches, bishop of Winchester. He was an important person and held high office under Henry III, but for some reason he had to leave court hurriedly. He held the benefice of Alton and was known to be the owner of land in many parts of the country. How he came to possess land at Shoelands is not clear, unless Henry III had made him such a grant when he was in favour. Nor do we know why he gave a carucate to Selborne. It is possible that it was to help the newly-formed Augustinian house at Selborne. This was a common practice of landowners in the 13th century, when a wave of religious feeling was passing over the country. Selborne Priory farmed the land, but it also set up a kiln for making encaustic tiles in the field opposite Shoelands, known today as Stickums. Kerry says that the clay used for making the tiles came from this field and the water necessary was supplied by the little stream which runs down to the river Holybourne.

In 1223 Ralph de Fay was succeeded by his son John. John died young and his mother Beatrix, the widow of Ralph, was given Puttenham as a dower. In these rough times it could not have been easy for a woman to be a landowner. She probably had many disputes with her subordinates and she certainly fell foul of the Church in some way, for in 1244, according to the Woods MSS., she was excommunicated and her lands were confiscated by direction of the King.[9] Why she was excommunicated we do not know, but she did not remain in this state for long, since in the next year her lands were restored to her. In 1246 Beatrix died and her only heirs were her two daughters. The Sheriff of Surrey was ordered to take into the hands of the King 'the manor of Puttenham and all lands which Beatrix de Fay held in Puttenham, which had been of Ralph de Fay formally her husband, to keep them safely until otherwise ordered by the King'.[10] The manor of Puttenham was eventually returned by the King to the two daughters of Beatrix de Fay and divided into two manors—Puttenham Bury and Puttenham Priory. Before turning to the history of these two manors it is possible to gain some inkling of the lay-out of the village at the death of Beatrix in 1246, when the whole of Puttenham belonged to the manor of Bramley.

We know that there was a church, from the middle of the 12th century, situated at the east end of the village, and that Turberti des Bosches had a house at a certain distance from the house of 'Solands'. The mention of 'Solands' and the ditch would lead us to suppose that there was a house of some proportions behind the 'ditch' or moat. Robert de Barevill had at least 30 acres at 'Solands' but, interesting though it might be, we cannot be sure that he resided in the house behind the 'ditch'. We get a glimpse of cruck houses built by de Barevill for his cottars, on the track leading from Seale to Puttenham. This was the old secondary trade route running along the lower slope of the Old Way, the Hog's Back; it was sheltered and well drained; thus it was an obvious situation for agricultural dwellings. South of this track was Rodsall, or Redessolham. Here there was certainly a steward's house, farm buildings and, possibly, a mill. This is all that it is possible to visualize, but the agricultural lay-out can be imagined, even if somewhat dimly.

The three fields, in which during these centuries the peasants of Puttenham had their strips, and in which the demesne was situated, can probably be identified. It is almost certain that one—the South field—lay down the 'Suffield Lane' of today. The land here is composed of good well drained soil and is very suitable for arable farming; Puttenham Common is near and available as common land for grazing the cattle of the manor. The old name of Suffield Lane, which is still used, suggests that here was one of the three fields, viz. South Field. An indenture of 1583 mentions a field at Rodsall called Horsmonde as 'lying in the Common Field',[11] and the will of Richard Tice, 1618, speaks of '1 acre in the Comon ffeild called South ffield'.[12] The second field, the Middle Field, may have been alongside the present Highfield Lane. One of the fields here is called Middle Field.[13] Again this is good arable land and, again, it is close to Puttenham Common—on the opposite side of the Common to the South Field. This field is on higher ground than the South Field, hence the name Highfield. In an indenture of 1619 Richard Tice

Draught oxen in the thirteenth century: South Field, Puttenham

transferred land to George Billinghurst, which included Great High Field, Nether High Field, South and North High Field and Common Field—all listed as lying up High Field Lane.[14] Again, in the will of Richard Tice, 1618, there is mention of '1 acre, 1 roode in the comon ffeilde called highefeild'.[15] It seems reasonable to conclude that these divisions were made from the old Common High or Middle Field. The third field is not quite so distinguishable, but the obvious place for it would be on the north side of the Street running up to the Hog's Back. Field names on the Tithe Map of Puttenham seem to support this view. They are Common Down Side and Bevil Common Down and the whole area is called Further Common Downs.[16] If we look again at the will of Richard Tice, we find that he leaves in his will 13½ acres in the 'comon ffeilde called north feild'.[17] If these positions are accepted then it is probable that the earliest houses along the Street were those of the villeins and cottars from the time of Domesday onwards. From their doors the manorial workers could go straight out to their own strips, or to those of the demesne, depending on whichever fields were in cultivation. On these fields the ordinary rotation of crops was carried out as in other villages in Surrey. Besides these cultivations, however, as has been stated, there is evidence that Puttenham grew vines. Apart from this not uncommon crop at this time, the village followed the accepted manorial pattern of farming—working the fields and grazing in common and living in houses, whether small or large, in a state of discomfort which would appall us today.

NOTES

1. G.B. Gosling, 'Notes on the History of Puttenham', fol.1–MS. in the possession of the Puttenham & Wanborough History Society.
2. Woods MSS. Godalming Hundred, vol.17, p.173.
3. Ibid., p.245.
4. Guildford Muniment Room, MS. 11/5/35.
5. G.B. Gosling, 'Notes on the History of Puttenham', fol.1.
6. Ibid., and *Surrey, (V.C.H.),* vol.iii, p.53.
7. Woods MSS., Godalming Hundred, vol.17, p.206.
8. Kerry, vol.iv, p.88.
9. Woods MSS. Godalming Hundred, vol.17, p.177.
10. Ibid.
11. Guildford Muniment Room MS. 70/35/7.
12. Woods MSS. 'Collections', vol.4, p.112.
13. The Puttenham Terrier of 1765 speaks of this part as 'Middle Field'.
14. Guildford Muniment Room L.MS. 349/127.
15. Woods MSS. Collections, vol.4, p.112.
16. Guildford Muniment Room MS. PSH/PUT/13/1(1) and PSH/PUT/13/1(2).
17. Woods MSS. Collections, vol.4, p.112.

III

THE MANORS OF PUTTENHAM PRIORY AND PUTTENHAM BURY

BY THE END of the 12th century, however, changes were appearing in the manorial pattern. The original manors which appeared in Domesday were, in a number of instances, divided. Sometimes they were separated into two or more manors under the overlordship of the original lord and became sub-feudatory manors, as in Compton, where five manors appear at the end of the century, including Eastbury manor, Westbury manor and the manor of La Felde, all under the lordship of the de Windsor family. Sometimes the manor was divided into two as in Godalming—the King's manor and the Rectory manor, both acknowledging the Bishop of Salisbury as their overlord. Although division was often the case there were exceptions, for the Bishop of Winchester maintained the manor of Farnham intact. Puttenham, however, seems to have followed a policy of its own for, although it was divided into two manors on the death of Beatrix de Fay—Puttenham Bury and Puttenham Priory—there was not a common overlord as at Compton or Godalming and two sub-manors were attached to Puttenham Bury, those of Rodsall and Shoelands.

As we have seen, in 1246 Beatrix de Fay, the lord of the manor of Bramley and Puttenham, died leaving her lands between her two daughters. Philippa de Neville took Bramley and part of Puttenham, which became known as Puttenham Bury named after the most conspicuous point—Bury Hill at the east end of the Church. Matilda was given the remainder of Puttenham. Philippa, with the help of her husband, perhaps, was able to cope with the problems of a lord of the manor, but Matilda, a widow, either as a result of an unequal struggle or because of the influence of religious fervour in the 13th century, passed her lands over to Newark Priory, which already held land in Compton and the manor of Hurtmore.[1] The records of Newark show that Matilda levied a fine on the Prior of Newark in the Court Baron on his taking possession of the property in 1248.[2] The Prior was to hold the lands by one tenth of a knight's fee in chief to the King and, by virtue of this, the Prior of Newark retained the right of frank-pledge which enabled him to judge in cases of misdemeanour. With this division of land the manors of Puttenham Bury and Puttenham Priory were formed. The manor of Puttenham Priory only occasionally appears in the picture, but it is possible to follow more closely the fortunes of the manor of Puttenham Bury and its lords during the next 150 years under William de Wyntershull and his descendants.

The de Wyntershulls were large landowners who increased their holdings by marriage and by purchase. When they appear on the Puttenham scene, William de Wyntershull, the head of the family, is a man of great importance. The *Surrey Place Names* gives his ancestral home as at Wintersell's Farm, Byfleet, and his own home at Winterhill Farm, Worplesdon. Cecilia, Lady Boston, says Winters Hall, Bramley,[3] was another of his places of residence. It is probable that he moved round his manors and lived off each in turn, for he appears to have lived at Wield in Hampshire at some time and his daughter was married in the church there. [4] His own marriage brought him the manor of Bramley which was extensive and included Puttenham Bury, since he married Beatrice the daughter of Philippa Neville, who had been left these lands by her mother Beatrix de Fay.[5] William, however, was not just a landowner; he was a true Anglo-Norman administrator. At one time he was Seneschal for the manor of Farnham and, as such, represented the Bishop of Winchester. This appointment necessitated his being at Winchester a great deal, but he would often come to Farnham to meet the manorial officials and he always presided over the Hundred Court. In 1266 he was one of the signatories of the confirmation of the Farnham Charter which granted Farnham 'some of the rights which belonged to the bishop' of Winchester.[6] He had his own suite of rooms in the castle[7] and, next to the bishop, he was the most important man in the town. He was also Steward of the Household of Henry III.

In spite of his duties as Seneschal and Royal Steward William seems to have had time to attend to his personal affairs and possessions. In 1251, three years after he became lord of the

A knight in the thirteenth century: Puttenham Common

manor of Puttenham Bury, he confirmed the grant of land at Shoelands to Selborne Priory which had been made by Peter de Ryvall in 1235.[8] The rent which Selborne paid for this was a gold spur, due on the day of St. John the Baptist. In 1270 he obtained for himself and his heirs 'free warren in his demesne land in Frollebury' (Frosbury) in Puttenham. This practice ensured fresh protein in the shape of rabbits for the lord's table, since no one else was allowed to kill a rabbit, and it was the duty of a warrener to see that offending villagers were brought to justice. Bearing in mind the speed with which rabbits, or conies as they were called, increase this warren would be a menace to the gardens and strips near it. Furthermore, any enclosure of common land would reduce the amount of ground on which the villagers could graze their stock. However, it looks as though the warren remained, for at a Quo Warranto held in Guildford in 1279 the jury presented that 'William de Wyntershull had warren in Potenham, but by what right they did not know'.[9]

Puttenham Bury, however, was not the only manor with which he was concerned. In 1257 Aylmer de Vallence, Bishop Elect of Winchester, who was always in need of money, conveyed two carucates (two hides) in West Wield in Hampshire to William de Wyntershull;[10] in Compton in 1272 de Wyntershull secured the manors of Westbury and Polsted and the advowson of the church for £120.[11] No doubt he had lands at Byfleet and certainly at his manor of Worplesdon which needed his attention.

In 1287 William died 'on the Wednesday before S. Gregory being seized in right of his wife, Beatrice, daughter of Philippa Neville and sister of John de Fay, of 50 acres of arable land in Puteham, value 9d. an acre, 2 acres of meadow at 12d. an acre and 8 acres of pasture at 4d. an acre'.[12] William was followed as lord of the manor of Puttenham by his son Walter and then by a bewildering number of Thomas or William de Wyntershulls until in 1400, 'on the Monday after Epiphany', the last male heir of the de Wyntershulls died. He left his manors to his two sisters, Alyns and Joan. Joan, the widow of William Weston, took Puttenham Bury and Alyns took Bramley, so from now onwards these two manors were separated.[13]

The first William de Wyntershull was an interesting man, evidently one of great ability and character. He was obviously anxious to increase his possessions in land, which in those days meant not only wealth in real estate, but a manor was of great assistance to the lord's housekeeping expenditure. Not only was his own family dependent on him, but he had a considerable household of attendants, secretaries, servants, all of whom had to be fed. Therefore, if he could move from manor to manor and live off each one in turn his problem of maintenance was greatly eased. This was obviously de Wyntershull's practice. When he came to Puttenham he would have found his rabbit warren a useful source of protein. It is possible to imagine this haughty Anglo-Norman—lord, landowner, administrator—moving through the village finding fault here, commending there and representing law and order. There is no record that his successors followed his example as representatives of the strong Norman ruling class; but, as time went on, the power of the lord of the manor faded and he became the owner only of a farming estate.

The information regarding the manor of Puttenham Priory is much more difficult to discover and, when it appears, less colourful. There is no record as to how much land Matilda, the second daughter of Beatrix de Fay, received on her mother's death; we know that the Prior had all the rights of local administration and in 1347 an Inquisition held in Guildford states that in Puttenham Priory it was found 'that the Prior (of Newark) had and still had in the ... township of Puteham lands ... and there had been no subsequent change'. The document continued with the statement that the Prior claims 'assis, panis and cerviss in manero suo de Puteham'.[14] This is not explicit as to the extent of the manor or its boundaries, but it does indicate that there had been no alteration since 1248. The land given by Matilda to the Prior carried a grange, which later became known as the Priory. It should be noted, however, that there was never a monastic establishment here; the house was probably that of the Prior's steward.

In 1296 a new name appears—Frollebury—which later became Frosebury or Frosbury. Frollebury was probably a sub manor of Puttenham Bury and may have been the home of an independent farmer. The first reference to it is in 1296. We find that 'William Frollebury and his wife Joan had two messuages of land in Potteham which they held of Thomas, son of William Frollebury'.[15] One messuage was almost certainly for a house and this is the first indication of Frosbury house. Its successor stood in the grounds of the present manor house and was pulled down when the rectory (the present manor house) was built in 1824.

By the end of the 13th century we can get a clearer view of the village. Leaving Shoelands, protected by its moat, and walking eastwards we would probably pass the field where the encaustic tiles were made, the vineyard and the house of Turberti des Bosches. On our left is the common field lying between the road and the Hog's Back (to give it its modern name); on our right is the Middle or High field and beyond this the Common. Coming into the Street we find on both sides the houses of the villeins, with farm buildings behind each, and the smaller cruck houses of the cottars. At the east end of the village stands the church, a small rectangular building with a belfry, but no tower. We might even meet the rector, Henry le Sigher, who could have been watching the building of the Lady Chapel or the extension of the chancel, both of which were completed by the end of the 13th century. Passing the church on the south side we come to a house which has just been built by William de Frollebury and his wife Joan. Retracing our steps past the church we take the track which passes the South field, the third common field, and come to Rodsall, which is now occupied by William le Paumer. Thus the village may have appeared at the end of the 13th century.

By the first half of the 14th century the manorial system was showing signs of disintegration, although it cannot be said that there was, as yet, any danger of it breaking up. Commutation of villein services for money payment was increasing rapidly, but this did not mean the complete independence of the manorial agricultural worker. Commutation helped both the lord and the labourer. The lord could, as a result, hire labour merely when he wanted it and the villein could no longer be forced to leave his own fields to work on the demesne. It is obvious that farming for profit was soon to supersede farming for subsistence and the social structure was on the eve of change. Soon the villein with initiative was going to make every effort to buy his land and would become the yeoman farmer; those who had not this initiative would become the landless agricultural workers. This movement may have been accelerated by the Black Death, but it was not initiated by it, since there were other important reasons for the break up of the manorial system.

The first half of the 14th century was a period of intermittent famine, of plague and of unrest. It was not until the end of the reign of Richard II that the pattern of the future emerged and agricultural policy became clearer. The famine of 1315-17 affected the whole of Europe, including England. Days and weeks of rain made harvesting almost disastrous and, as a result, the seed for the next year was poor and scarce. In 1317 things were even worse and the corn yield was a mere pittance. Floods followed in many places with the inevitable result—famine. The stock, also, was in a poor state as murrain, which had appeared in 1274, was killing sheep and cattle. The villeins were forced to get in the demesne harvest, such as it was, before they could attend to their own strips, and there was no opportunity for them to segregate their healthy stock from the diseased cattle and sheep belonging to their neighbours. It became plain that the future lay in farming in severalty.

Soil exhaustion was another factor which undermined the manorial system of rotation of crops. This was evident before the disastrous years of 1315-17. Owing to lack of food it was possible to keep only a minimum of stock through the winter, which meant that very little manure could be obtained for the land and only the demesne benefited from grazing on the stubble. The villeins were forced to put their beasts on the lord's land, not on the common fields, as soon as the harvest was over; and the common fields were often ploughed, according to the reeve's direction, before they could be grazed and so manured. The land, therefore, became more and more exhausted and the one year fallow was not sufficient to restore it. Lords of the Manor experienced land starvation long before the Black Death and were willing to accept commutation for services which would ensure a certain income. Villeins, anxious to escape manorial despotism, were buying their land, generally on a stock and lease rent. This was especially so in the small villages and would, almost certainly, have taken place in Puttenham.

Professor McKisack states that the Prior of Tooting leased his manors from 1322;[16] at Haslemere enclosures were made on an increasing scale at this time;[17] in Leatherhead there were reported to be 12 freeholders in 1336. As early as 1249 John de Gatesdon leased to Nicholas Malemeins his 'Manor of Compton with appurtenances' for his own life at a yearly rental of 10s.[18] This is an early example of a lease for life and in 1291 Margaret Camoys leased 'for life only' lands in the manor of Eastbury, Compton.[19] In Farnham in 1256 Aylmer de Valence, Bishop Elect of Winchester, 'feeling the urgent need of ready money' let 103¼ acres of the best land in the demesne to tenants and in the same year all customary work was commuted.[20] This was wholesale freedom from villeinage for the manorial worker on the estate of the Bishop of Winchester. Obviously the manorial system was breaking up before the Black Death struck this country and there is little doubt that the same process was going on in Puttenham.

The first indication of any encroachment on the manor of Puttenham Bury seems to have been when William le Paumer of Rodsall obtained a 'lease for life of a messuage and ½ a virgate of land in "Potenham" in 1273. William and his heirs for ever to render yearly 4s. and one rose to John son of William'.[21] The reference to a rose is interesting, since a rose is still given yearly to the lord of the manor of Seale (the present owner) by the occupants of a 17th century house on Rodsall land. In the same year there is reference to a further alienation of land when John le Cotte, or Cutte, gave 'an estate', including a water mill, to 'John le Paumer as the marriage portion of his daughter Juliana'.[22] It is permissible to think that William le Paumer was anxious to extend his possessions at Rodsall by acquiring Cutt Mill on the marriage of his son John to Juliana. But his ambitions were thwarted when Juliana, widow of John le Paumer, gave the mill to Henry le Sigher, rector of Puttenham, and in 1319 conceded to him the 'right and claim' for 40s.[23] Henry le Sigher would have had strips in the common fields as the peasants had, but, apparently, he hoped to add the proceeds of the mill scot to his income from agriculture and tithe. Much later, in 1347, the mill appears in another inquisition. This time it is a bondsman and his wife buying land: 'Robert de Holm and Joan his wife, bondsman and bondswoman ... acquired certain tenements in "Potenham" from Henry le Sigher of the yearly value of 6s. and 8d'.[24] A villein appears here to be buying land for himself, on what kind of lease is not stated, but obviously, Robert de Holm was hoping to become a free tenant of the manor. His tenancy was probably the mill, as a little later the family of Homly appears to be in possession of the mill which had been sold by Juliana to Henry le Sigher.[25] We know that freeholders were established in the manor of Puttenham Bury in 1347. In an inquisition held in the 20th year of Edward III to discover what land in 'Potenham' Thomas de Wyntershull held in fee of the King on his death in 1340, it was stated that he received 103s. in rent from free tenants.[26] These examples show that there was a definite move by the villeins to consolidate their holdings by leases, or by marriage portions, or by purchases, as in the case of the Holms, or by whatever means the freeholders may have obtained their lands from Thomas de Wyntershull.

This gradual movement towards free tenure continued during the second half of the 14th century and was accelerated by the increasing labour troubles after the Black Death and, in Surrey, the process was probably added to by the assarting of woodland.[27] Labour shortage and mobility of the population in rural areas, which appeared after the Black Death, increased the demand for freedom. In Puttenham, as elsewhere, we shall see that the villeins took every opportunity to secure their release from manorial ties. There is no direct evidence that Puttenham was affected by the Black Death, although neighbouring places such as Esher, Haslemere and Farnham suffered.

After the plague of 1349 rents began to rise and so did agricultural prices. This tendency increased after the second outbreak in 1361; therefore the farmer aimed at augmenting the rent roll as well as looking for profit on agricultural commodities. The answer for the lord was sheep farming, or renting his land to former villeins. The landowners of Esher and of Godalming began to specialize in sheep, as did the monks of Waverley Abbey in Wanborough, but in Puttenham the lords of the manor rented land to the villeins as small farms. There is ample proof to indicate that the manorial system was dying here and that the time of small enclosed fields was approaching. Harvests during the 15th century were, on the whole, very much better and this encouraged the more enterprising villein to try his luck alone.

It has been noted that there were a certain number of free tenants in Puttenham before the Black Death. From 1360 their number began to increase. Some would rent land, stock and buildings from the lords and others would only rent land. They would hire their labourers and would fence their arable and pasture fields; only the common land would remain open to all, and even that would be nibbled at by the farmers. According to Thorold Rogers the leases were not long—perhaps only for a life–but the farmer had advantages which he never enjoyed under the manorial system, for he could determine his own farming policy, he was not tied by manorial services, and he could will his property if the lease had not run out.

The references to purchase of land are very human documents. The villein who had decided to strike out on his own must have given a great deal of thought to his venture. After all, he was giving up the security of the manor, even if his tenure had been bounded by service, and, if his life might now be free, he had to make his own future and justify his action to himself and his family. These men were adventurous. During the 15th century this change from agriculture in common to agriculture in severalty was continuing in Puttenham, and continuing successfully, it would seem–land was bought, leased and willed. In 1426 Roger Bulbek of 'Potenhm̃' granted to 'William Follebury ... all those lands and tenements in the Parish of Potenhm̃ which he had lately purchased of Richard Pychord and which the said Richard lately purchased of Thomas Este of Potenhm̃'.[28] In 1487 'Richard Legart of Ponteham' left his house, garden, lands and tenements to his wife, Alice.[29] This would not have been permissible under manorial rule. Again, in 1442 lands which had belonged to Thomas Cranford, clerk, were given to John Dessante of 'Potenhm̃'.[30] Among these documents one interesting entry suggests that legal advice was sought in such land transfers–'Simon Ulrich citizen and barbour of London and his wife assigned Philip Taillow of Potenhm̃ as their attorney to deliver to John Lygeard of Clendon ... certain lands lying in Potenhm̃'.[31] During this century men in Puttenham were not only starting on independent farming, but they were, as their returns increased, anxious to add to their prestige. Accordingly, they built timber framed houses in the village street. Today there are three, namely Winters Farm, the Old Cottage and Rosemary Cottage which date from the 15th century. These are all houses which must have been built by prosperous independent farmers. The fact that during the 15th and 16th centuries a number of houses of this type were built in the street supports the view that the Puttenham farmers relied on arable and not on sheep farming–there would have been no room for so many resident farmers to run sheep on Puttenham land.

In spite of their seeming independence, most of these farmers, together with all the agricultural workers, had still to abide by certain manorial restrictions–such as the lord's right of heriot, wardship, escheat, etc. The Court Baron undoubtedly functioned in the manors of Puttenham Priory and Puttenham Bury, although the first reference to it is nearly 200 years later. Thus we have no record of what took place there in the 15th century, but by referring to the Customary of the Manor of Farnham, 1617, we can imagine the cases which were dealt with in Puttenham. 'The lord ... shall have wardship and marriage of his free tenants'; 'Of ten pounds from James Beale for the marriage of the heir of William Parker'[32]; 'The wardship of Richard Dervassel, a tenant, is committed to John Neve until the age of sixteen years'[33]; 'William Hampton forfeited one messuage and one virgate ... for waste in felling oaks'.[34] The lives of the labourers hired by the tenant farmers were probably hard, but in a monetary economy they could go elsewhere if they wished. By the end of the 15th century the tenant farmer had, in many cases, become a man of substance with more comfort in his home, enjoying a higher standard of life, and above all, freedom. The manorial system had almost disintegrated and the yeoman farmer was now ready to enter the Tudor age, to enjoy its excitement, and to take part in its spirit of adventure in agricultural policy.

NOTES

1. Cecilia, Lady Boston, *The History of Compton in Surrey,* London 1933, p.109.
2. Woods MSS. Godalming Hundred, vol.17, p.178.
3. Op. cit., p.75.
4. Olivia Mills, *Wield Parish History,* privately published 1965, p.26.
5. Woods MSS. Godalming Hundred, vol.17, p.175.
6. E. Robo, *Mediaeval Farnham,* Farnham 1935, p.181.
7. Ibid., p.132.
8. Woods MSS. Godalming Hundred, vol.17, p.206.
9. Ibid., p.184.
10. Olivia Mills, *Wield Parish History,* privately published 1965, p.26
11. Cecilia, Lady Boston, *The History of Compton in Surrey,* p.75.
12. Woods MSS. Godalming Hundred, vol.17, p.184.
13. Ibid.
14. Ibid., p.180.
15. Ibid., p.236.
16. May McKisack, *The Fourteenth Century 1307-1399,* (Oxford History of England vol.5), Oxford 1959, p.329.
17. G. Rolston, *Haslemere in History,* Haslemere 1956, p.12.
18. Cecilia, Lady Boston, *The History of Compton in Surrey,* p.88.
19. Ibid.
20. E. Robo, *Mediaeval Farnham,* pp.87-88.
21. Woods MSS. Godalming Hundred, vol.17, p.224.
22. Ibid.
23. Kerry, vol.ii, p.96.
24. G.B. Gosling, 'Notes on the History of Puttenham', fol.16.
25. Ibid.
26. Woods MSS. Godalming Hundred, vol.17, p.186.
27. R.H. Hilton, *The Decline of Serfdom in Medieval England,* London 1969, p.22.
28. Woods MSS. Godalming Hundred, vol.17, p.247.
29. *Surrey Wills (Archdeaconry Court. Spage Register),* Surrey Record Society, vol.v, No.xvii, London 1921, p.69.
30. Woods MSS. Godalming Hundred, vol.17, p.247.

31. Ibid.
32. *Customary of the Manor of Farnham,* trans. by Elfrida Manning, Farnham Museum Society 1967, pp.3 and 4.
33. Ibid., p.4.
34. Ibid., p.7.

IV

THE CHURCH AND THE RELIGIOUS LIFE OF THE PEOPLE IN THE MIDDLE AGES

THE CHURCH of St. John the Baptist, as it stands today, is a representative example of ecclesiastical architecture and furnishings through the centuries. The earliest evidence of its existence is architectural—the Norman pillars, as was noted earlier. So we can accept the fact of a 12th century church in Puttenham. The question is bound to arise, however, as to what religious life existed before the church was built and who built it. Inevitably there must be considerable conjecture in answering this.

In the 7th century England was divided into vast dioceses, so that it was impossible for the bishops to give detailed consideration to the evangelizing of the countryside and to the maintenance of services in these wild districts. Consequently, minsters were built and were served by priests and laymen who were sent out into the immediate neighbourhood as missionaries. These minsters generally included a church, sleeping quarters, workshops, farm buildings and a wall surrounding the whole for fear of attack from heathen tribesmen. The buildings would usually be situated by a stream or a spring for use in baptism. All Christian parents were expected to bring their children here to be baptized. From these minsters the priests and laymen would penetrate the rough countryside. They would stop at a cross, which had already been erected, probably on an old pagan site, and would preach or hold mass for those who came to hear them. As they evangelized so they would push further afield and gradually little chapelries would be set up where once there was only the preacher's cross. The minster, however, would remain the mother church.

There was a minster at Tuesley, which served the Hundred of Godalming; this Hundred contained Redessolham and the later Puttenham. It is almost certain that Redessolham and Puttenham were christianized from Tuesley and it was there that the children were taken for baptism. These religious communities, or minsters, are found in many parts of England, for example, in Kent, in the South West, and in the Midlands, and, nearer at home, at Farnham and they all followed the same pattern of evangelization. Hence it is not far-fetched to think of this part of West Surrey as having been converted to Christianity from Tuesley.

One of the duties of the travelling priests was to discover pagan centres dedicated to a heathen god and to which the people were accustomed to go for worship. Here the priest would set up a cross and would substitute a Christian service for a pagan one. In Puttenham there is the possibility of a heathen centre which became a Christian place of worship at Church Croft, a small hill not far from an Iron Age camp, which is approached by a network of tracks and paths. The name Church Croft has no significance in later times as it was never church property, but there must have been a reason for it. Could it have been an altar which had been erected to some god and where a preaching cross was later set up? There is no direct evidence to support this, but as no church is mentioned in the Domesday Survey of Rodsall, and as Church Croft is near to Rodsall, it is permissible to think that in the time of Tovi, the Saxon, it was the religious and Christian centre for the manor and that it was served by priests from Tuesley.

Although in Surrey the minsters seem to have held their own in the religious life of the rather sparse population of the 9th century, yet churches were being built as more land was cleared. These churches were, in the first instance, of wood, although later the local stone was used. It was usually the lord of the manor who built such a church for the use of his family and his manor. He looked upon it as his private property and appointed his own priest. By the end of the 10th century these manorial churches were superseding the minsters and, whereas from the minster the priest had been an occasional visitor for the purpose of conducting services in the open, with the erection of a church the priest became resident in the parish and, even if he was responsible to the lord, he was counted as one with the villagers.

It is not possible to discover whether the church at Puttenham is older than the middle of the 12th century. It is not mentioned in Domesday, as many churches of Saxon origin are not, but this is only negative evidence and the date must be decided by the Norman arches of about 1160. Almost certainly it was a manorial church, probably built by one of the de Fays, lords of the manor of Bramley and Puttenham. The lord of the manor appointed the priest and in Puttenham he appears to have retained this right until 1307, when the advowson was given to St. Mary-without-Bishopsgate, a priory which owned considerable amounts of land in Wonersh and other parts of Surrey. The lay patrons of the manorial churches seem to have found the appointment of priests a burden, so that by the end of the 13th century the monastic institutions were taking over advowsons and the financial gain which went with them.

During the 13th century changes in the worship and the structure of the church took place which reflected changes in theological belief. In early Norman times the interpretation of Christianity mirrored the crudities of life and death and men were obsessed by the fear of hell. By the end of the 13th century the understanding of religion had been mellowed by the monastic ideal and the flowering of the intellectual renaissance, and had been softened by the invocation of the Virgin Mary. The institution of the feast of Corpus Christi had a profound effect. As a result of these influences the Lady Chapel was built at the end of the north aisle of Puttenham church, as was commonly done elsewhere. The chancel was extended which removed the celebrant further from the people in the nave, thereby stressing the distinction between priest and layman and heightening the element of mystery in the mass. By the 14th century the inhabitants of the villages were learning more of their religion through the preaching of the Friars. Offerings from pilgrims and, later, dues from the fair provided the means to beautify Puttenham church. This was the age of decorated architecture and painted glass. The people of Puttenham marked this change by building a transept and inserting decorated windows which gave more light than the Norman windows had provided. Celebration of the mass became more frequent and an altar was placed in the transept, although no dedication is known. In 1402 the building of the tower was begun. This was a feat of some magnitude, but when it was finished, probably early in the 16th century, Puttenham was seen to be dominated and apparently protected by its church, which stands on a hill at its east end, overlooking the Street and the houses.

In spite of the sense of security which the tower and the church must have given to the villagers, the 15th century was a time when gloom and retribution were the key-notes of religion. The villagers believed that their salvation depended upon the Passion of Christ; consequently the rood hanging over the entrance to the chancel helped them to remember the sacrifice on the cross. As a result, in the 14th and 15th centuries devotion to the sacrifice and the belief in the Real Presence was fundamental to their religion. The mass was the centre of their worship. According to the canons of King Edgar in 960, the priest was to celebrate the Eucharist (or mass), visit the sick and, if necessary, give them Extreme Unction, baptize the infants and observe Sundays and feast days. These duties of the parish priest were his primary ones, but he had to live. Accordingly, he was an agriculturalist and had to work his strips (his glebe) in the common field and graze his cattle on the waste land. He had a certain amount of income derived from tithe—if he was a rector he would receive the greater tithe on corn and the lesser tithe on other productive commodities. He could expect certain dues, such as mortuary fees (soul-scot) and plough-scot—a small charge levied on each plough at Easter. He did not owe dues or work to the lord, since his glebe was freehold.

The Sunday services which the laity might attend were mattins, mass and evensong; mattins preceded mass and evensong came 'after mete'. Longland in Piers Ploughman says people ought to attend all the services, but probably they only went to mass and then not to receive communion, except once a year at Easter. In fact, their attendance gave them an excuse to meet their friends in the only place possible outside their own little hovels. Their attitude was quiet and at solemn moments, when the sanctus bell rang, they would kneel in adoration. To them the church was somewhere where they could feel safe from the daemonology in which they still privately believed and from the hard world in which they lived.

However, the church was not only a place of worship for the villagers: the nave was also their village hall. Here was their meeting place and here they brought their tithes. Also, the church was the centre of such activities as the fair, the church ale or the mystery plays and, as the church was arbiter in legal matters, wills would be witnessed by the clergy and often proved before the high altar. The secular use of the church was very important to the village.

It is not possible to fit individual priests into the story of

Puttenham. Almost certainly they followed the general pattern of parish priests. Occasionally the veil is lifted for a few moments. Henry le Sigher, 1272, is the earliest incumbent known to us. We do not know who appointed him; probably it was the lord of the manor. His successor was Robert, appointed by the Hospital of St. Mary-without-Bishopgate in 1307. The register of the Bishop of Winchester tells us that later in this year he was ill—Robert 'being old and infirm the custody of his person and of the rectory was committed to Walter de Shalford, presbyter, he accounting to the Bishop for the profits and duty'.[1] There are now names, but no personalities until 1400. In that year Edward Cranford was instituted. His brass lies in the chancel and shows him in eucharistic vestments. It was he, in all probability, who organized the building of the great tower. For this, materials had to be brought from Guildford and Godalming and the large stones from Ash. Cranford must have been a man of character and determination to be responsible for this task.

In 1502, when Richard Quinby was rector, Richard Lussher of Shoelands died and left money in his will to build a rectory at the east end of the church and gave lands to maintain it. In return he asked to be buried before the altar in the Lady Chapel and that masses should be said for his soul at this altar every year. The Lady Chapel, therefore, became known as the Lussher chantry. In 1507 George Mitchel was instituted as rector and, although he remained as incumbent until 1533, his character does not seem to have been beyond reproach. In 1521 William Lussher complained in the Star Chamber that George Mitchel did not administer divine service as he ought to do and that he was an evil liver. A further complaint was made that William Lussher and Thomas Jenkins when walking on Guildown, were met by Mitchel who called Jenkins a 'Welsh Horse'. Jenkins, who was probably Lussher's servant, drew a knife and attacked Mitchel. As a result, it was said, Lussher dismissed Jenkins.[2]

In this last half century before the Reformation people had become more conscious of their church and of their responsibility towards it. Furthermore the 15th and early 16th centuries were a time when the fear of death and damnation was very real. This fear is apparent in the tremendous increase in propitiatory masses and masses for the dead. The wills of the period also emphasize this attitude and they help to give a picture of the religious life of the period. In almost all of them there are special bequests to the churches and these express the type of worship at the end of the Middle Ages. As late as 1485 Richard Shorter asks 'to be buried in the churchyard of St. John the Baptist, Putnaham. To the mother church of Winchester 2*d.* To the light before the Cross in the church of Putnaham one sheep ... residue to Joan my wife.[3] In 1487 Richard Legart of 'Pouteham' made provision by his will 'To be buried in the churchyard of St. John the Baptist, Pouteham. To the church of St. Swithin, Winchester 2*d.* To the upkeep of the light of St. Mary one sheep. To the light of the great cross one ewe ... '.[4] Billinghurst of Rodsall provided for a trental of masses to be said for his soul.[5] From these wills and that of Richard Lussher several points arise. They show how important were the propitiatory masses and candles before the altar and the rood; they indicate that there was such a rood in the church at Puttenham, although there is no architectural evidence that this was so; they are examples of how animals were left to the church in payment for some privilege (these animals would be farmed out by the churchwardens for a fee); and, lastly, they emphasize the immense influence which religious observances still had on the people of the later Middle Ages. But changes were approaching and medieval Puttenham was to emerge from its isolation and be affected by national movements both in its religious and secular life.

Before we turn to Puttenham in the time of the Reformation let us consider the position of the village in respect of its place in the surrounding district. There is no definite evidence of the amount of travel or of the conditions of the roads in medieval Puttenham, so to what extent the village was connected with the outside world must be a matter largely of conjecture and comparison. Earlier we saw how tracks were made and used by the waves of prehistoric immigrants who cleared the scrub and settled in the forests south of the Old Way. These same tracks were almost certainly used by medieval man and are recognizable today in the deep cut lanes leading to the village, such as the Seale road or Murtmore lane. Puttenham, like Seale and Compton, never developed as Guildford and Farnham did. Their geographical position did not lead to their growth into market-towns; this does not mean, however, that these villages were isolated, rather it is certain that people moved about quite freely. They came and went through these villages for

Wayfaring in the fifteenth century: Puttenham Heath

all manner of reasons, but they left them as they found them—small agricultural communities.

There can be little doubt that the condition of the roads which connected villages with the outside world were bad in the 15th century, in comparison with our lanes of today. The Roman roads still existed, although in a state of decay, whilst a vast network of smaller tracks had grown up, joining town to village and serving the agricultural countryside. Probably a great many of these were little more than bridle paths; faulty construction and lack of drainage made travelling very difficult, especially in the winter. The decay of the monasteries, such as Selborne, and the break up of the manorial system meant a progressive decline in the care of the roads. In the Paston Letters we are continually reminded of the danger of riding along roads in such bad repair and of the fear of attack by robbers.

In spite of the hazards of travel, however, there was probably a very large amount of wayfaring life. Lady Stenton writes, 'from the evidence which can be collected about the use of roads in medieval England the conclusion grows that for all but the heaviest transport they served men well'.[6] Prof. May McKisack considers that communications were eminently possible, if difficult.[7] There were pilgrimages of all kinds, not only to Canterbury; the Hundred Court was held once in five weeks; fairs attracted a large number of people from the countryside around; and there were the ordinary day-to-day movements connected with agriculture. The usual form of travel was on horse-back and the average distance of a horseman was 30 to 35 miles a day. Goods were moved in 'long carts'; this was a slow process, but it enabled farmers to take their goods to market and, by the 14th and 15th centuries these markets were increasing in numbers. Carters and carriers were regularly employed on certain routes to carry parcels and letters; throughout the Paston Letters it is apparent that there was such a service at frequent intervals from Norwich to London. Not only people used the roads but also all animals; every kind of stock, from cattle to geese, was driven to market along the lanes or the main roads.

Bearing in mind this large amount of wayfaring life it would be surprising if there was not considerable movement on the lanes in Puttenham. These lanes, which run down from the Old Way, connected up the villages along the greensand. These were the

Seale lane, Puttenham Hill and the Downs road and the people living in the villages saw the wayfarers as they passed through. Many a time, they must have noticed Chaucerian pilgrims making their way to some shrine; or have watched the stall holders at the fairs taking their properties and their goods to the one-day fair of St. John the Baptist at Puttenham, or to the bigger fair at Shalford. Not only would they have watched the fairmen pass, but many of them would have joined their neighbours, who were setting out for one of the great events of the year; with them might be monks and friars moving along the lanes on the business of Selborne or Newark Priory. In the 15th century tenant farmers from Winter's Farm, the Old Cottage or Rosemary Cottage (to give them their modern names) would frequently fill their heavy carts or load their pack horses with farm produce and set out for the market in Guildford or Farnham. There they would meet other farmers and would discuss the agricultural future as they do today. The carriers in their journeyings would connect village to village. Probably the drovers did not bring their cattle through Puttenham; their way lay through Wanborough and along the Hog's Back, but they added to the large movement that there was along the lanes of Puttenham. It is obvious that the village was not isolated, but the traffic was local or else in transit. Geographically Puttenham could not offer any inducement for settlement, such as important cross roads, river fords, or a direct route to the coast. It was just an agricultural entity and as such it would remain, in spite of the picture which Piers Ploughman and the Chaucerian poems give us of a large amount of wayfaring life in South East England. Through the centuries which followed this traffic continued. Puttenham watched it and noted it, but did not change its agricultural way of life, based on its fertile soil and its village community.

NOTES

1. Quoted by Kerry, vol.2, p.129.
2. P.R.O. Star Chamber 2/17/86 and 2/18/11. Information kindly supplied by Mr. S.R. Christophers.
3. *Surrey Wills (Archdeaconry Court. Spage Register),* Surrey Record Society, vol.v, No.xvii, London 1921, p.13.
4. Ibid., p.69.
5. Woods MSS. 'Collections', vol.1, p.42.
6. D.M. Stenton, *Medieval England,* Oxford 1958, p.207.
7. *The Fourteenth Century 1307-1399,* May McKisack, p.314.

V

PUTTENHAM LIFE IN THE SIXTEENTH CENTURY

WHEN WE COME to the Tudor period it is obvious that England is entering on a time of excitement and adventure. In the intellectual, political and religious spheres there are great changes—the New Learning, the Royal Supremacy, the Reformation, and the opening up of the New World. Puttenham, in common with the rest of England, could no longer sleep in isolation. The village was bound to be caught up in the current of events and to feel the stirring of the new ideas which were abroad.

For the first few years of the century there was probably little alteration, but by the second decade changes in the village appear which indicate improvement in the lives of the yeomen, at least. Independent farmers were prospering now that they could follow their own agricultural policies and not be tied to that of the lord of the manor. As they became more wealthy so they wanted more comfort and they built themselves farm houses of considerable size—Hook Lane Farm, Farm Cottage, Street Farm (as they are called today) were built between 1520 and 1550. Behind these houses were the farm buildings, consisting of barns, cow sheds, ox stalls, perhaps a stable if the farmer worked with horses, bake house, dairy and beyond that a salting house. These buildings show how independent the farmer, working his land in severalty, had become. In the Street there were still the houses of the manorial workers, who as yet cultivated their strips in the common fields. But gradually they abandoned their strips and became hired labourers and the modern labour pattern thus appeared. This process could be seen everywhere. In Compton during this period a steady progress was made towards independent farmers served by paid agricultural labour.[1] In Godalming the movement was towards sheep farming. Dr. W.C. Palmer considers that by 1630 'almost the whole population must

House building in the fifteenth century: The Street

have been engaged in the cloth industry in one way or another'.[2] He continues with the statement that there were probably 5,000 sheep grazing on the Peasmarsh. Many of the clothiers must have been wealthy men, as is testified by some of their houses which still stand in the High Street.

There is no reference to large scale sheep farming in Puttenham. There are several reasons for believing that here this kind of agricultural policy did not obtain. There is no documentary evidence to substantiate the view that sheep farming existed, but the proof lies in the number of houses built in the Street in the 16th century, which obviously belonged to well-to-do farmers. There was not sufficient land for the owners of these farms to run sheep in any number and, further, a look at the fields today shows them to be small and surrounded by banks. It is thought that these small banked fields are due to couch grass being heaped up at their edges. This grass has always been a pest to Puttenham farmers; they raked it up by harrowing in an effort to get rid of it, and the harrows deposited the couch at each end of the field—the distance between the two banks being never more than 400 yards; this distance might have been dictated by the fact that the oxen, which were used for ploughing, could not go more than about 400 yards without a rest and it would not be economic to allow them to rest before they deposited the couch grass. Hence small banked fields were formed which must have been arable and could never have been used for running sheep in any quantity.

The Tudor farmer was quick to take advantage of any improvement in agriculture and a new farming policy soon appeared. It was no longer one of subsistence, but was now based on the profit motive. Markets were opening, roads, if to us little more than tracks, were generally negotiable and Guildford, Farnham and Godalming could be reached without trouble. It was also possible to look even wider than these three markets, since river traffic was now becoming common and corn was often sent to London. The cattle of England were by this time recognized on the Continent as good beasts and farmers now made every effort to keep them through the winter, although the use of roots as winter feed had not yet been discovered. Crops had changed little since the 14th century, but more trouble was taken with ploughing. A new development was the beginning of hop growing in England in 1552. The first reference to the crop in this district was at Farnham in 1597. The improvement in building and comfort which appear in houses of the yeomen in the Street of Puttenham show that the farmers were quick to take advantage of the increasing agricultural prosperity.

In the Street, also, the artisans were building better houses for themselves and we can read of some of these men in the Wood MSS., e.g., 'John Byknor, Weaver' who, in 1552, 'made red cloth for John Chuter',[3] and 'John Mott, Taylor', who appears in a transfer of land to 'John Whitt, Wheelrite',[4] and it is permissible to think that there was a housewright (i.e. builder-cum-architect) who was responsible for the many houses which were built in the village at this time. Also, somewhere in the Street there was an ale house. A certain George Lussher of Witley, in 1534, went into an ale house in Puttenham called *Avenell's House.* Here he heard a conversation between Henry Biknor, Shirer, and some other person, about their proposal to murder John Biknor. Later, when questioned as to what conversation had taken place between these men over their ale pots, he said he had heard nothing 'for he drank his drink and went his way'.[5] However, Henry Biknor murdered Shirer and then hanged himself, but John Biknor was left in peace to weave his red cloth. The Biknors seem to have been a pugilistic family, for in the Wood MSS. we read that, in 1560, in the *George Inn* in Guildford there was a quarrel between two Puttenham men—Chitty and Biknor, on the one hand, and a third party, not named, on the other. Chitty and Biknor apparently chased the unnamed man into the street and 'made an assault upon him, break his head with a dagger and then went to run away with his hors'. It is not stated which Biknor this was, nor what was the sequel.

By the middle of the 16th century the ordinary villager found himself involved in national defence. During the Middle Ages military service was the responsibility of the landowner, who held his land by half or quarter of a knight's fee, but when invasion appeared imminent then each tithing had to produce trained bands, armed, at the demand of the Lord Lieutenant of the County. This would only be in times of danger, as, for instance, when there was a fear of invasion in 1583. The tithing man, or constable, was responsible for supplying the number of men demanded, for sending them to the muster with the parish arms and armour and for providing them with the stipulated amounts of money for their maintenance. The men selected were yeomen.

They were paid 8d. a day from the tithing of Godalming, of which Puttenham was a part, and they had to go to Guildford to attend the muster. The pikemen had only to produce their weapons for inspection, after which they could go home. Gunners had to be trained in skirmishing and the use of their guns for two afternoons. The Loseley MSS. give details of the Puttenham men who were ordered to attend the muster held in Guildford in 1582—in a 'List of the Company of ffoote within the Hundred of Godalming'. 'Putnahm̃' sent '4 pikemen selected', '3 Bill men selected', '7 Bill men of the Beste sorte', '16 Bill men of the seconde sorte', '4 Archers selected', '3 Gunns'.[6] With this company went Wollward, the rector. After being inspected in Guildford by the Lord Lieutenant, they returned to Puttenham, except for the '3 gunmen' who stayed for one afternoon's training. The company, on reaching the village returned their arms to the constable, who stored them in the church, according to custom. The Loseley MSS. also record 38 men mustered from Puttenham in Elizabeth's reign, although the actual date is not given.[7] In this list some of the men appear to be unarmed. They are 'Smythes, John Snelling, five labourers and moneers'. Perhaps these formed an early R.A.S.C. Also there is a reference to Bartholomew Hardings and John Billinghurst who are designated as surveyors.[8] Today, with our nuclear arms and highly skilled armed forces, this little band of untrained villagers seems singularly inadequate to help in putting up a defence against an invading army, but they were part of the only force which England could raise, even at the time of the Spanish menace.

The early Tudor period was a time when monastic manors disappeared with the dissolution of the monasteries and when laymen purchased the lands and manorial rights and became resident in the villages. This sequence can be seen in all parts of England, in the North and in the South, in village and in town. Everywhere the old gentry were taking advantage of the monastic decline and were consolidating their own lands and establishing their position in the country. The manors of Compton were bought by the More family—Westbury by Sir Christopher More in 1545, Polstede by Sir William More in 1558 and Hurtmore by Lord de Windsor on the dissolution of Newark Priory.[9] In Godalming the Town manor was bought from the crown by Sir William More, who built his beautiful Elizabethan house at

Loseley. Puttenham was no exception; the family which gave this village the first resident lord of the manor was that of the Lusshers.

The story of the Lusshers is traceable from the 15th century, when they began consolidating their possessions. It is probable that the Lusshers came from Devonshire, but they certainly invaded this corner of Surrey and, especially, Puttenham. They appear in Compton and Witley; they are connected with Selborne and Waverley; they are resident at Shoelands; they become lords of the manor of Puttenham Priory and Puttenham Bury, and several are buried in the church of St. John the Baptist. For 120 years their name is synonymous with Puttenham. There is not very much evidence as to the family, but every now and then the curtain is lifted and we can see that their story is similar to that of other laymen who were taking over the manorial lordships from monastic institutions all over the country.

The first reference to the connection between the Lusshers and Puttenham appears in 1462, when Richard Lussher rented Shoelands from Selborne Priory. This would be the old moated house which lay behind the Shoelands house of today. In 1484 Thomas Lussher, his son, was paying a rent of 100s. to Selborne Priory for Shoelands.[10] Thus the Lusshers had made a firm entry into Puttenham. Almost immediately after Thomas Lussher had rented Shoelands, Selborne Priory was dissolved; there is no evidence that Thomas then bought Shoelands, but it seems probable, as the family continued to live there.[11] Now the story switches to Waverley Abbey. In the Abbey records 'William Lussher of Shoelands' appears as its last steward at a stipend of £2 13s. 0d. p.a.[12] William held this post at the dissolution of Waverley; he must have had an anxious and busy time dealing with the King's Commissioners, although he does not appear to have suffered himself.

Meanwhile, the Lusshers appeared in Compton. A William Lussher was tenant of Westbury Manor in 1472. He seems to have been a tough customer; he was summoned by the lord of Eastbury manor on a charge of seizing six of his oxen. In the following year another summons was issued, since Lussher 'with force of arms broke into Richard de Brocas's close at Compton and carried away his trees and underwood growing there to the value of 30s.' Again he was summoned for cutting down more trees 'by force of arms,

A sixteenth-century bedchamber

to wit, staves and knives'; he and his men broke into the close and carried off '100 oaks and 100 cartloads of underwood'.[13] Obviously William Lussher of Compton did not do things by halves!

At the end of the 15th century Sir Richard Lussher of Shoelands appears as a benefactor to Puttenham, for it was he who gave money and lands for a parsonage. Next we find the Lusshers in Cheam. Robert Lussher, son of William Lussher of Shoelands, was living in Cheam in the late 1530s and in 1541 he came into the Puttenham picture, when he bought the manor of Puttenham Bury. This was part of the manor of the de Wyntershull's, which passed to Edmund Pope, who sold it to Robert Lussher;[14] in 1545 Robert Lussher bought the second manor, Puttenham Priory.[15] Owning Shoelands and now the two manors, the Lusshers had taken over Puttenham and the monastic influence of Selborne, Newark and Waverley had gone—the manorial rights belonged to a layman.

The extent of the two manors in 1544 is not known, but in 1587 the acreage appears considerable—'30 messuages, 30 cottages, 12 tofts, 4 mills, 10 dovecots, 60 gardens, 60 orchards, 200 acres of land [probably arable], 20 acres of pasture, 100 acres of wood, 1,000 acres of heath and furze and £5 rent'.[16] The rents were probably paid by independent yeomen and the manor almost certainly extended outside the boundaries of the village into Compton and Elstead. The value of the manors was put at £9 15s. 9d. for Puttenham Bury and £6 16s. 8d. for Puttenham Priory.[17] There is no doubt that there was little land in the village that was not owned by the Lusshers, and by this time they were certainly wealthy landed gentry. Yet their home conditions appear very simple to us. The will of Jane Lussher, wife of Thomas Lussher of Shoelands, which was proved in 1559, gives us a glimpse into the house of a 16th century landowner. She left to her 'nevye, Nicholas Lussher, the hangings and belongings to the hall, savinge the cupboard, also the hangings in the great chamber', and to her son 'Willyam Lussher, the gylte salt without a cover and the things in her chamber'.[18] If these belongings were considered worth specifying in a will, her other possessions could not have been of much value!

The Lussher saga must be carried on until the early years of the 17th century. So possessive a family would not permit their story to be rounded off neatly at the end of the 16th century. Robert Lussher, who had bought the manor, died in 1545 and his widow re-married, but she astutely kept a financial interest in the manor for her son's sake.[19] He, Nicholas Lussher, was a minor, so the lands reverted to the Crown until he became of age, but we hear nothing of him until his death in 1566. It is then that we learn his wife's name and the fact that his son was left a minor on his father's death.

Nicholas Lussher lived at Shoelands and when he died he was buried in the Lady Chapel at Puttenham with his forebear, Richard Lussher. His wife, Mary, erected a stone memorial to him containing a brass and his coat of arms carved above.[20] this remained in position in the north wall of the chapel until the 1860s, when the influence of the Camden Society was let loose in the church and the stone was removed, the brass disappeared and the head of the memorial was placed under the organ. Here it was found in later years, but was thrown under a hedge in the churchyard. In 1969 it was rescued from there and placed in the south porch. So once more, the memorial to Nicholas Lussher has returned to the church where he is buried. The son of Nicholas, confusingly Nicholas also, came of age and entered into the Lussher inheritance and held his court as lord of the manor in 1591;[21] but tragedy struck the Lusshers in 1603 and 1604. In 1603 three of their children died within a few days of each other and were buried in the Lussher tomb the day after the death of each. In less than a year his wife, Dorothie, died and was buried the same day.[22] In 1868, during alterations to the chapel, the graves were opened and it was found that the bodies had been buried in lime and that bay leaves were scattered inside the coffins,[23] indicating that the mother and her children were victims of the plague, which was severe at the time of their death.

It might seem that Nicholas Lussher had little more use for his home and his position after the death of his wife. In 1609 he sold his lands and his manorial rights of Puttenham Priory and Puttenham Bury to Sir Oliph Leigh, a kinsman, for £5,500.[24] In 1616 the old house of Shoelands lying behind the moat was forsaken and the present Shoelands was built.[25] Puttenham was thereby given a 17th century brick house—one of the most beautiful in the village. This story of the Lusshers is reminiscent of the Pastons' gradual accumulation of lands in Norfolk. Then the

Lusshers, as the Pastons, fade into the mists of history.

Whereas the Lusshers were landowners busily increasing their acres, the Billinghursts were yeomen, tenant farmers, who may have secured their independence from manorial farming during the 14th century, and have enclosed their fields and become successful farmers. Thus they are typical of the independent yeomen farmers of the 16th century. It is only possible to get random glimpses of them and they usually appear as the Billinghursts of Rodsall. The family name is found in Godalming, Shackleford and Seale, but there is no evidence as to the connection the families may have had with each other. The first reference we have to the Billinghursts in Puttenham is in 1503, when William Billinghurst of Rodsall was assessed for an aid of 5s.[26] This amount would indicate that he was a man of some substance. In 1508 it is known that the Lusshers held Rodsall,[27] and so the Billinghursts must have been tenant farmers. In 1568 William Lussher had 'a rent charge of lands in Rodsall'[28] showing that the Lusshers, not the Billinghursts, were the owners of Rodsall. In 1569 and 1573 John Billinghurst was ordered to appear for muster 'as a bill of the beste sort'.[29] As the men selected for muster duty were always yeomen we can assume that throughout the 16th century the Billinghursts of Rodsall were tenants of the Lusshers.

Let us return to the first William Billinghurst, who was assessed for an aid in 1503. The next reference to him is his will in 1522 which seems to have caused dissension in his family. First he asked to be buried in 'Puttenhm̃ churchyerde' and gave 'xxd.' to the work of 'makyng the stepill tower of Puttenhm̃'. This last bequest suggests that the tower, begun early in the 15th century, was not yet completed, more than a hundred years later. William continues —leaving to his sons John and Richard 'oxen, bees and kine ... except a sufficiency to the prson', this latter probably being a mortuary fee; to his son Henry '2 pans and a cauldron'.[30] These household utensils were often mentioned in wills. They were very acceptable when cooking pots were scarce in every kitchen, necessitating stews as the main part of every meal. The meat and vegetables could in this way be cooked in the same pot. Useful undoubtedly, but these cooking pans could not have been so valuable to Henry as the farm stock of oxen, bees and kine left to John and Richard. He soon decided to leave Rodsall, where he had been living with his father, and go to Shackleford where another brother, Robert, who got nothing from his father's will, was farming.[31] Presumably Henry took his two pans and his cauldron with him. Meanwhile, John farmed Rodsall and Robert farmed Shackleford, both of whom were successful; but Richard, who shared the stock with John, 'fell into poverty'. He was nevertheless allowed 'meate and drinke at his brother's table'.[32] Henry and Richard seem to have been the unlucky members of the Billinghurst family. Robert 'Byllynghyrst' died in 1545 and he, like his father, asked in his will to be 'beryed in the churcheyerde of puttenhm̃'. The witness to this will was 'William Rodley clarke and prson of Potenham',[33] whom we shall meet later.

Henry Billinghurst appears to have been successful in his farming, in spite of leaving Rodsall and going to Shackleford, since his sons Edward and John Billinghurst at a tax assessment in 1551 were charged 10s. each on goods worth £10 and, later, in 1559 at 25s. on goods worth £25.[34] It looks as though the sons made farming pay. Edward appears to have had a dispute with the Lusshers in 1548 with regard to a claim made by them on lands at Rodsall; consequently Edward made 'fences against Lashmere' (Lussher).[35] John Billinghurst's death was one of the first recorded in the new church register of 1562.

During the 17th century the Billinghursts still appear as yeomen, but the reference is now to Frosbury. 'George Billinghurst ... sick in body' leaves 'to the poore of the paryisshe church in Puttenham 20s.' and 'to my kinsman ... the lands called the mannor of ffrosbury'.[36] This will was proved in 1628 and shows the change in attitude to the church and to religious ideas. No longer does the testator leave money to pay for masses to be said for his soul, nor was money left to the church either in Puttenham or in Winchester, but the charitable bequest was for the benefit of the poor. George, John or William Billinghurst appear often in the church register in this century, always they are described as yeomen and as such appear as billmen in the musters.

There is nothing remarkable about the Billinghursts nor is there anything exciting in their story: they are just ordinary inhabitants of Puttenham leading a hard but independent life and are typical of others who will appear later—the Tices, the Fludders and the Tofts. It was these yeomen who were the mainstay of Puttenham and, together with those in other villages, the backbone of England.

The Reformation ended the religious outlook of the Middle Ages and the isolation of village communities. The abandonment of the doctrine of transubstantiation, of propitiatory masses, of communion for the laity in one kind only, called in question the old beliefs in which the villagers had been brought up, and made them realize that they could no longer live in their own small circle: they were caught up in events and movements which affected the whole country.

Professor Dickens points out that by the late 1530s there was a movement away from the traditional form of wills, which shows a trend from the old medieval religious conception towards a more Protestant outlook.[37] This can be seen in the wills of some of the parishioners of Puttenham; but under Mary there was a reaction which appears very clearly. We have already noted the medieval background to the wills of Richard Lussher and William Billinghurst; others followed the same form. In 1530 'John Estmũde' left '111 lambs to the rood and St. John's Lights'.[38] In 1536 'John Ede of Putman' asked to be 'beryed in the church yerde of the parysshe Church' and left 'to the high Aulter of the Parysshe Church of Putnam viiid.'[39] These show the medieval thinking of the testators in their mention of the veneration of the rood and the saints. However, in 1545 'Robert byllynghyrst of the pyshe of piuttinhm̃ to be beryd in the churche yerde of puttehm' left 'oon shepe' to each of his 'Godchydren' and to 'Thoms merest both my ffarmes in the pyshe of puttenhm̃'.[40] This will is entirely secular. Under Mary, when there was a return to the old services, reaction also appeared in the wills. Thus, 'Edmund Lee' of the 'peshe of Puttnham to the churche of Puttnham 2s. and a taper to be set before the Roode, to the poor people iiis. iiid. to pray for my soule'.[41] This was in 1558. A year earlier John Billinghurst of Rodsall had ordered 'I will that there shall be ffive masses with diriges said at my burial'.[42] However, when we come to the 17th century we find that money was often left to the church, but for such things as additions to the structure. For example, in 1634 Francis Wyatt of 'Putnam' left £5 'towards building a gallery in Putnam churche or otherwise towards repairing and reedifieng the church'.[43] By this time, also, the poor were frequently remembered. In 1628 George Billinghurst 'sick in body' left 'to the poore of the parysshe church of Puttenham 20s.'[44] There is no mention of candles or masses for the dead now; the Protestant element had triumphed.

Unfortunately there is no means of telling what was the reaction of the villagers to the numerous Acts of the Reformation Parliament, but there can be little doubt that they realized that changes from without were being imposed upon them. In 1535 Henry VIII ordered his commissioners to tour England and to enquire into the financial state of every church, so that he might know how much money he might expect from the first fruits and tenths. William Rodley was rector of Puttenham at that time and he, with incumbents elsewhere, must have had to make a return, but there is no record of what that was. The Royal Injunctions of 1536 ordered the Bible in English to be placed in the choir of every church, and both the Royal Injunctions of 1536 and 1538 enjoined the reading of it by everyone. It was undoubtedly read, as the Act of 1543, which tried to limit the reading to the gentry only, forbade the reading of it by apprentices, serving men and artificers and even women. The reason for this was the prevalence of 'crafty, false and untrue' translations, including that of Tyndale, which were prohibited to all.[45] It is likely that those parishioners who could read would enjoy some quiet moments with the Bible in the choir of Puttenham church, until 1543 at least.

Probably the first pointer which would have been recognized by the villagers with regard to the approaching changes, was the news that Waverley Abbey had been suppressed in 1536, to be followed by the dissolution of Newark Priory in 1538. Selborne had gone much earlier, in 1480. From now on all monastic lands were under secular control in Puttenham, as elsewhere in England.

In 1547, the hand of the State came down heavily on Puttenham in the shape of the Chantries Act. This Act was a definite step towards a more Protestant outlook; it ordered the dissolution of all chantries, as being used for superstitious purposes, and the confiscation of chantry lands and money. Puttenham could not escape. The Lussher chantry-chapel was dismantled, and the rectory together with certain lands was seized, since they were part of the chantry bequest. An extract of the return by the Commissioners who carried out the Survey of Puttenham lands is interesting. It states that these lands consisted of three fields—Great Piece and Little Piece in 'Rodsaull', a field in Gildowne and the 'parsons croft and garden', this last being the rectory. It continues 'there be neither woodes nor underwoodes growing upon one crofte of lande in Puttenham containing iii acres neither upon one acre of land lying upon Gyldowne ... The yearly rent of these lands to maintain the lights in the chantry was xis. viiid.'[46] This reference illustrates the thoroughness with which the Commissioners went about their business. In their conclusion the Commissioners did not consider that the return from the fields 'will do more than maintain the boundaries and enclosures', so they valued them at 'xs.'[47]—slightly less than the church valuation.

In 1549 the new Prayer Book was sanctioned by Parliament; it came into use on Whit Sunday, 9 June. It was ordered to be read in every church and it would be invaluable to know what was the reaction of the congregation in the church at Puttenham. The changes in worship were not entirely revolutionary. The late medieval doctrines of the sacrifice of the mass and of transubstantiation were rejected, but a doctrine of the Real Presence was retained together with the main structure of the medieval mass.

Further intrusion of the State into the religious life of the people was carried out in 1549. Edward VI ordered Commissioners to make an inventory of all valuables in the churches. In 1552 a further inventory was ordered and in 1553 it was commanded that these treasures were to be seized and only one chalice and one patten was to be left for the incumbent with 'a sufficient stock of surplices', for, 'the King's majesty had need presently of a mass of money'. We have a copy of the inventory of 1552 for the church of St. John the Baptist at Puttenham, which shows that it possessed, among other items, a chalice and patten 'of sylver', vestments, surplices, 'aulter clothes', 'a red canype clothes of Brydyes satin' (probably a canopy borne over the sacrament in procession and made of Bruges satin), four bells in the steeple, and a saunce bell.[48] On the same day, 6 October 1552, the Commissioners went to Wanborough, Compton and Seale and made similar inventories. There is no record of the actual confisaction of these 'goodes', but there is no doubt that it took place after the survey, as was the case in other churches which had been visited by the commissioners. At this time, also, statues, figures of saints and the rood screen were condemned with much of the medieval decoration in the churches. It must have been hard for the incumbents and their parishioners to accept this vandalism as well as the new Prayer Book, but just when they had begun to get used to the changes in worship and churchmanship the 1549 Prayer Book was withdrawn and a more Protestant one was substituted in 1552. Whether this ever reached Puttenham is not recorded; its introduction was followed very soon by the death of Edward VI, so that it cannot have been legal for more than 15 months. However, there is mention of it being used in Shere Church, not many miles away. In the churchwarden's accounts for 1552 there is an entry 'Whereof paid for the book of Common Prayer 4s.'[49] It is, therefore, probable that it was used in Puttenham church.

The next five years, 1553-58, under Mary Tudor, were a time of reaction; in fact, it is possible that it was a relief to the villagers of England to return to their old services, as it would be to many in England today to go back to the liturgy of 1662. An example of how easily the country slipped once again into the old ceremonies appears in 1556 when the body of Stephen Gardiner, Bishop of Winchester, was brought from London to Winchester for reburial. Between 23 and 29 February 1556 the procession wound its way through South East England and passed along the road from Puttenham to Seale. Obsequies were held en route and 'a carte laden with torches and scochins' preceded the cortege and money was distributed to 'the curates and clerkes' of every parish along the way, of which 'Putnam' was one. We read that 'All these curates and clerkes of the churches when the corps was coming, the[y] stood in the way in their best ornaments and honourably received the same by adding their oraysons and prayers ... and devoutly served the corps as it preceded, every parishe churche has iijs iiijd and money given in every place to the poore where the[y] came'.[50] Neither these 'oraysons' and prayers, nor the procession would have been allowed in the reign of Edward VI. Matthew Ryle was the rector of Puttenham at the time of the funeral procession. He had been appointed in 1554, so it is probable that he was a man who had readily accepted the return to the medieval form of worship; one can imagine him standing in his 'ornaments' at the south gate to the churchyard, receiving the money distributed from the 'carte' and making his oraysons and prayers as the cortege passed. The description of the procession together with the evidence of the wills of this period indicate a return to the old worship under Mary and we can assume that the medieval mass was said once more in Puttenham church.

More changes, however, were imminent at the accession of Elizabeth in 1558. Again the people of Puttenham had to adjust their religious life at the dictates of the State—and not only the small village of Puttenham, but all England. The worship of pre-Reformation times had gone for ever and the country was to become Protestant. By Elizabeth's Act of Uniformity of 1559 a new Prayer Book was introduced; this was largely based on that of 1552, and severe penalties were imposed for failure to use it. A fresh change of churchmanship was enforced, services became less centred on the sacraments and the emphasis on the Word became more marked. The effect of these changes can be seen in the church of Puttenham. Any furnishings which might be connected with so-called medieval superstitions were removed, here as elsewhere, and the Lord's Prayer and the Ten Commandments were painted on the wall behind the altar at the east end for all to see; the repainting of the letters is an item which often occurs in later Puttenham churchwardens' accounts. If the rood still remained, as seems most likely jùdging by the wills of Mary's reign, then it was taken down at this time; there is no mention of it later on. The Church of England was now set on a steady Protestant course and the Elizabethan religious settlement, though modified later, remained the basis of *Ecclesia Anglicana.*

The successive rectors, from the institution of William Rodley in 1533 to the end of the century, are interesting. Rodley was the first incumbent to be presented to the living by a layman, Henry, Lord Montacute; until this date the advowson had been in the possession of St. Mary-without-Bishopsgate. This change of patron did not mean any change in the services which Rodley would conduct, but the shadow of approaching reform was apparent and, as rector, he had a troublous time ahead of him. He was the incumbent in 1535 and had to give details of his income and that of his church to Henry's Commissioners; it was he who had to arrange for the Bible in Latin and English to be placed in the chancel of his church in 1536 and, during the latter years of Henry VIII, he must have been aware of further imminent changes. He was rector when the Chantries Act was passed under Edward VI (1547) and Puttenham felt for the first time the heavy hand of the State in religious matters. Rodley was forced to witness the dismantling of the Lussher chantry and the confiscation of the parsonage house. Whether he was allowed to continue living in the rectory as a tenant of the State, we do not know, but it is probable that he was. Next, he had to assist in the making of the first inventory of his church's treasures by the government Commission of 1549 and thereafter, with his churchwardens, he was responsible to the Justices for their safety. His troubles were not yet over, for he was to meet a violent death. The story appears in the Chancery Records in a rather obscure case brought by two men, John Reynard and Richard Serle, who sued Richard Bedon, Gent., for the murder of Rodley and the theft of his belongings. Reynard and Serle claimed that they were Rodley's executors and, as such, responsible for his possessions. Bedon's defence was that Reynard and Serle were not Rodley's executors and that when he, Bedon, heard that Rodley had been murdered in Compton, he ran to the rectory to secure Rodley's belongings from theft. The Chancery Records do not supply the end of the case or state who was the murderer, but the fact remains that Rodley was dead.[51]

There now followed four incumbents and two curates in ten years. One of the curates, John Kerry (or Kere), is said to have been a monk of Waverley. The curates were put in charge of the parish during interregnums and there appears to have been an unusual number of 'clerks in charge' of Puttenham at this time. The cause may have been either the official changes in religion or the general shortage of clergy. During the changes in religion in the middle of the century the clergy were often too ignorant to preach. However, from the accession of Elizabeth the rectors of Puttenham were men of education, since all were graduates of Oxford and Cambridge. The injunction that the clergy must read more was obviously taken to heart by the Revd. Henry Beedell, M.A., who became rector in 1598. He left in his will, amongst other books, the 'Book of Martyrs to my son-in-law and also to him Austen's Book of Statutes' and 'to the Vicar of Wittley Hooker's Book of Ecclesiastical Polity'.[52] Furthermore, towards the end of the century ordinands were coming from a better class of society. Henry Beedell was one of these. He was a married man and one of his sons succeeded him as rector of Puttenham; his daughter married the rector of Compton. When he was instituted there was probably no rectory for him and, obviously, he felt the need for a better place of residence, so he bought back the rectory which had been confiscated by the State in 1547 and lived there.

A complaint, by the clergy at this time, was that they were poor, that their income was not keeping pace with the rising prosperity of the time, and that they had to secure a plurality of benefices in order to have sufficient means on which to live. This was obviously the case with John Wollward M.A., who became rector in 1579. He had been a Fellow of King's College, Cambridge, but was dismissed because he insisted on taking the northward position when celebrating at the communion service. Who presented him to the living of Puttenham is not certain; he does not appear to have been in his parish for much of his time, as he probably needed more money than the stipend provided, and, consequently, secured the incumbency of Windlesham in addition to that of Puttenham, and was also made Canon of Windsor in 1572. These three appointments he held till his death at Windsor in 1598. He spent most of his time at Windsor, leaving curates to look after the parish of Puttenham for a pittance; probably he did the same thing at Windlesham. Three of the curates at Puttenham appear in the register and one, Henry Johnson, had three sons baptized here. In spite of the fact that Wollward was an absentee pluralist for most of his time, through him we can get a glimpse of the village as it was in the last quarter of the 16th century. One of the accepted duties of an incumbent was not only to supply arms for the protection of the realm, but also to serve with the muster. It is recorded in the Loseley MSS. that Wollward supplied arms along with the men of Puttenham and appeared in the muster parade at Guildford during one of the crises when it was thought that England might be invaded by Spain. And again, it can be surmised that if the Protestant Wollward was appointed to Puttenham then the parish was not averse to this type of churchmanship. It probably accepted the Elizabethan Settlement without question.

The story of the clergy as well as that of the religious developments and changes of the 16th century in Puttenham show that the village followed the pattern of the times. They depict it as a typical village reflecting the national background and the difficulties and hardships of the clergy who served the churches during the second half of the 16th century.

NOTES

1. Cecilia, Lady Boston, *The History of Compton in Surrey*, p.24.
2. W.C. Palmer, *Godalming*, County Branch Library, Godalming, p.4.
3. Woods MSS. Collections, vol.4, p.72.
4. Ibid., p.77.
5. Ibid., p.74.
6. *Surrey Musters:* Part I (taken from Loseley MSS.), Surrey Record Society, Number 11, London 1914, p.83.
7. Ibid., p.339.
8. Ibid., Part III, p.298.
9. Cecilia, Lady Boston, *The History of Compton in Surrey*, pp.86, 78, 117.
10. Woods MSS. Godalming Hundred, vol.17, p.208.
11. Kerry, vol.ii, p.156.
12. Kerry, *Waverley Abbey*, 1872, p.45.
13. Op. cit., p.94.
14. Woods MSS. Godalming Hundred, vol.17, p.187.
15. Ibid., p.212 K.
16. Ibid., p.193.
17. Ibid., pp.191 and 193.
18. Ibid., p.213.
19. Ibid., p.182.
20. Kerry, vol.ii, p.100.
21. Ibid., p.94.
22. Ibid., p.63.
23 Kerry, vol.iv, pp.122-125.
24. Woods MSS. Godalming Hundred, vol.17, p.194.
25. Kerry, vol.ii, p.157.
26. Woods MSS. Collections, vol.1, p.15.
27. *V.C.H., Surrey*, vol.iii, p.55.
28. Ibid., p.55.
29. Loseley MSS., vol.VII, quoted by Kerry.
30. Woods MSS. Collections, vol.1, p.15.
31. Woods MSS. Collections, vol.1, p.16.
32. Ibid., p.45.
33. Feet of Fines 21 Eliz., quoted by *V.C.H., Surrey*, vol.iii, p.55.
34. Woods MSS. Collections, vol.1, p.18.

35. Ibid., p.18.
36. Ibid., vol.4, p.21.
37. A.G. Dickens, *The English Reformation,* London 1964, p.192.
38. Woods MSS. Collections, vol.4, p.68.
39. Loc.cit.
40. Ibid., vol.1, p.46.
41. Ibid., vol.4, p.69.
42. Ibid., vol.1, p.46.
43. Woods MSS. Godalming Hundred, vol.17, p.229.
44. Woods MSS. Collections, vol.4, p.21.
45. An Act for thadvauncement of true Religion etc. (34 and 35 Henry VIII, c.1): *Statutes of the Realm,* vol.iii, pp.894-7.
46. Kerry, vol.ii, pp.163-4, quoting from a certificate relating to chantry lands in the Public Record Office.
47. Ibid.
48. Kerry, vol.ii, p.275.
49. *The Book of Reckoning and Other Memoranda, 1500-1612: the Church of St. James, Shere,* ed. E.R. Hougham, Guildford 1963, p.17.
50. G.B. Gosling, 'Notes on the History of Puttenham', fol.101.
51. P.R.O., Chancery Records, C/1/1316, fols.33 and 34. I owe this reference to the kindness of Mr. S.R. Christophers.
52. Woods MSS. Godalming Hundred, vol.17, p.249.

VI

PUTTENHAM IN THE CONFLICT BETWEEN CHURCH AND PARLIAMENT

THERE IS not much evidence of church life in Puttenham during the first 40 years of the 17th century. For almost a hundred years the incumbents were father and son—the two Henry Beedells. The father was rector from 1598 to 1636 and the son from 1636 to 1694. Both these men, who are remembered by a brass in the church, conformed to the new pattern of the clergy who were university graduates from Oxford with, it is hoped, ability to preach; they were probably men of a good social class since the father bought back the rectory from the Crown. It had been confiscated in the reign of Edward VI, but now the use of it as a parsonage house would give the rector more status in the village. Both Beedells left books in their wills, which gives the impression that they were men of some culture and, to comply with Laud's injunctions regarding church plate, the father gave the church a patten, the son a chalice.

There were many problems which faced the people in South-east England in the 17th century—plague, civil war and puritanism. Plague was always feared; it is recorded in several places in Surrey at the beginning of the century, including Guildford and Shere. It is no wonder, therefore, that it appeared in Puttenham since there was considerable movement of people between village and village. The Church Register of baptisms and deaths refers to it curtly and tragically in 1603—'at this time the pestilence was very rife'. Judging by the entries there were many more burials in this year than was usual: between January and May 1603 18 burials are recorded, that is, more than three times the average; we have already noted that Lady Dorothie Lussher and three of her children died at this time. It is easy to imagine the disruption which this pestilence brought to the life of the village.

Still greater must have been the disruption occasioned by the

Civil War. The South-east of England was almost entirely under the Parliamentarians, although Royalist forces held Farnham Castle for a short period and Basingstoke was a royalist stronghold until it was captured. Guildford, on the other hand, under Lord Onslow, was occupied by Cromwell's army. The small villages such as Seale, Puttenham, Compton and Peper Harrow were under Parliamentary administration throughout the war.

During the Civil War Phillip Mellersh, who was High Constable of the Hundred of Godalming kept an Account Book. From this it is possible to get some idea as to how the people fared at the time. Phillip Mellersh, lord of the manor of Farncombe, was responsible for collecting money and goods in the area of Godalming on behalf of the Parliamentary forces and for making his return to Lord Onslow at Guildford. The area he covered was only half the Hundred and included the villages of Compton, Tuesley, Peper Harrow, Eashing, Puttenham and Farncombe. The warrants were issued by Waller at Farnham and Onslow at Guildford. Mellersh had to collect money, horses, equipment, fodder, bread, cheese and other provisions, also, flock beds, coverlets and sheets. Occasionally a promise of payment for goods was made, but it is doubtful whether these promises were fulfilled. The requisitions fell on all the parishes under Mellersh's control.

In his accounts for February 1643 Puttenham was assessed at £3 12s. 11d. per week for 12 weeks.[1] On 11 May 1644 Mellersh wrote that Puttenham, with some of the other tithings, was 'full of soldiers', so he was not demanding a supply of hay and oats from there. The householders who were ordered to take billets were unable to refuse, but were given tickets stating the number of men quartered in each house and the duration of their stay. These tickets were supposed to be redeemed at a later date, but it is doubtful if they were ever honoured. Another entry on 4 January 1644 states that a 'warrant was issued by Lord Onslow for the supply of one dragoon horse from Puttenham'. Phillip Mellersh gives at the end of his accounts a summary of the charges he imposed on the villages and the return for Puttenham includes 1½ dragoon horses and trooper (the value of the horses would be divided among the villages, hence ½ a horse!), 1 hackney, 3½ teams and draught, £63 in cash, 50 lbs. of bacon, 17 doz. bread, 1½ cwts. cheese, 4½ loads of hay, 63 bushels of oats, 1,500 lbs. pork, 1 flock bed.[2]

This list of commodities, including a sum of money, which were requisitioned from Puttenham was heavy for so small a village, but it is typical of the demands made by the Parliamentarians on all the villages in the Godalming Hundred. In fact Phillip Mellersh's Account Book shows the crippling effect of the war on rural areas, even if they were not involved in any fighting. We can imagine the village full of soldiery, all billeted in the houses of the agricultural labourers. We can have sympathy with the housewife trying to feed unwanted lodgers and with her husband who had to contribute towards the £63 required by Mellersh. We can certainly sympathise with the small farmer who had to supply pork, hay and oats and with his wife who had to make the cheese and the bread and who might, also, be the unlucky one who had to supply the flock bed. It is just possible that Puttenham may once have been in earshot of gunfire. The legend is that there was a battle, or perhaps a skirmish, between Cavaliers and Roundheads at the top of Oliver Hill where it once joined the Hog's Back. There is no direct evidence of this, but Kerry says that two skeletons and some cannon balls were dug up there.[3]

One result of the Civil War was the great change brought about in church life by the rule of Parliament and the enforcement of Presbyterian discipline in all parishes under its control. In January 1648 an ordinance was passed by Parliament for dividing and settling the several counties of the Kingdom into distinct classical presbyteries.[4] The Prayer Book was suppressed, the Directory was substituted and Anglican priests either conformed or went into hiding. Thus church life as the village knew it, with the now traditional Prayer Book services came to an end under Puritan discipline and the villagers, who would have known little of the rights and wrongs of the two opposing sides, must have felt that their world was collapsing about their ears—that, indeed, as the Church Register records it in 1641:[5]

> About this tyme, began ye wars and then disorder. This Register being not carefully kept till ye happy restoracion of King Charles ye 2nd which was in ye yeare 1660 Mai 29th.

The Long Parliament soon began its work to overthrow Laudianism and to introduce Presbyterianism. In 1641 it ordered the placing of the communion table in the body of the church, the removal of altar rails and such furnishings of the church as might be termed superstitious. Permission was also given for establishing

Parliamentary troops in Puttenham

lectureships for the better instruction of the people. The Directory superseded the Prayer Book and in 1648 the Lords and Commons approved an Ordinance 'for the speedy dividing and settling the several counties of the Kingdom into distinct classical presbyteries and of congregational elderships'[6] and a tract was published referring to Surrey—'The Division of the County of Surrey into six Classicall Presbyteries, together with the names of the ministers and others fit to be of each Classis'.[7] Classis was the term used for the local meeting of ministers and elders. One of these six classical presbyteries was that of Godalming: 20 villages were contained within this classis, including Seale, Compton and Puttenham. Six Puritan ministers are named for this classis. One of them would have had Puttenham, among other villages, in his charge—perhaps Mr. Wood of Peper Harrow or Mr. Fortrey of Godalming. Most of the ministers were men who had been to Oxford or Cambridge and it would be reasonable to suppose that they were capable of teaching the villagers. To assist the ministers, 12 laymen were nominated as fit to serve as elders in the Godalming classis. Again, we do not know to whose charge Puttenham was given—perhaps tc Mr. Lickford of Seale. Revd. Dr. Geoffrey F. Nuttall, in a paper read to the Puttenham and Wanborough History Society, doubts whether the Godalming classis ever really got off the ground. This possibility is further substantiated by the fact that only two Anglican clergy within the area covered by the Godalming classis were ejected—Samuel Stileman from Farnham and Samuel Wickham from Pirbright. Nor is there any trace of nonconformity in Puttenham *after* the Restoration. Puttenham and Dunfold were among the 15 parishes in Surrey which were reported in 1669 as having no conventicle.[8]

In spite of the lack of evidence as to whether a classis really operated in the Godalming area, it is obvious that the villagers were forbidden to hold their traditional services, which they had now enjoyed for nearly a hundred years and the fact that the register was 'being not carefully kept' indicates disruption and distress. It is probable that the rector, Henry Beedell, did not leave the parish, nor was he ejected. In 1650, and again in 1653, one of his daughters was baptized in the church. He may have remained in retirement, taking no part in the services. The fact that the baptism of his daughter in 1650 is the only entry in the register for that year suggests that it may have been carried out in secrecy and possibly entered later. No matter how we view this period of Presbyterian discipline, it must have been a sad time for the people of Puttenham who had experienced the requisitions of the Parliamentary army and then were deprived of their customary devotions.

Henry Beedell appears again as rector in full control after the Restoration and there is no mention of any difficulty which he might have had with the remains of nonconformity in the village. Only one name occurs in this connection. In 1679 Caleb Woods of Puttenham, when 'chosen to be one of the Ale Tasters of Guildford, for refusing to take the Oath of Admittance into that office', had 'his goods taken by Distress to the value of £1 10s. 0d.'.[9] Woods was a Quaker and we shall hear of him later. There were other instances of Quakers in Puttenham in the 18th century–the baptism of Joseph Round, a Quaker, and the burial of three Quakers named Daniels. These are said to have come from London originally. Beedell remained as rector until 1694, in which year he died at the age of 84. Both he and Puttenham had survived the Civil War and the Commonwealth and once more the village concerned itself with parochial matters, having had enough of outside interference.

NOTES

1. F.G. Mellersh, 'The Civil War in the Hundred of Godalming', in *The Surrey Archaeological Collections,* vol.lxi (1964), p.61.
2. Ibid., pp.74-5.
3. Kerry, vol.iii, pp.104-109.
4. W.A. Shaw, *A History of the English Church during the Civil Wars and under the Commonwealth 1640-1660,* London 1900, vol.ii, p.16, n.3.
5. Puttenham Church Register in the Muniment Room, Guildford: PSH/PUT/1/1.
6. W.A. Shaw, loc. cit.
7. Ibid., vol.ii, pp.431-5.
8. 'Puritans and Nonconformists round Puttenham and Wanborough, 1640-1690'–a paper read to the Puttenham and Wanborough History Society by the Rev. Dr. Geoffrey F. Nuttall, May 1969.
9. Walter MacDonald Wigfield, *A Short History of Friends' Meeting, Godalming, Surrey,* Godalming, n.d., p.6.

VII

THE LORDS OF THE MANOR IN THE SEVENTEENTH AND EIGHTEENTH CENTURIES

WHEN THE LEIGHS purchased the manors of Puttenham, not for agricultural purposes but largely as a financial investment, they were only following the fashion of the period. Sir Oliph Leigh bought the manors of Puttenham from Sir Nicholas Lussher in 1610 and he himself was certainly interested in the agricultural aspect of his purchase. His estate was described as partly consisting of 'a great common or waste containing 500 acres in which he' (Sir Nicholas Lussher) had 'set burrows for coneys and erected a house for a warrener'.[1] In 1623 Sir Oliph Leigh was involved in litigation on the subject of his 'Rabbit Warren',[2] but by 1624 Sir Francis Leigh, the heir to Sir Oliph, had let the manors to Sir William Mynterne and from that time the Leighs seem to have had little interest in their inheritance, except as a financial proposition. This fact appears clearly in the life of a later Sir Francis Leigh, who was lord of the manor from 1675 to 1710.

This Sir Francis Leigh inherited lands not only in Puttenham, but in other parts of Surrey as well. He had also acquired property in Shrewsbury from Richard Sherer, a member of a well known Shropshire family. It was not long before Francis Leigh began a series of mortgages on both his Surrey and his Shropshire estates. The history of these financial transactions is shown in a case heard at the Bar of the House of Lords on 13 February 1727.[3] The reason for and the result of this case will be shown later. Meanwhile from it we learn that in 1683 Leigh mortgaged his Surrey property to Elizabeth Worster, widow, for £530, repaying £250 of this a little later and then borrowing a further £200 from her.[4] Still being 'in urgent occasion for money' he then mortgaged his Shrewsbury property. In 1688 he was ordered by the courts to repay his debt to Elizabeth Worster in the Common Dining Hall of the Inner Temple. By 1689 the sum was not paid and an indenture entitled E. Worster to 'take possession without let or hindrance' of Leigh's estates in Surrey.[5] However, Leigh was saved by Sir Robert Dashwood, Bt. of Oxfordshire, who took over the mortgage from Elizabeth Worster. In 1691 Sir William Cranmer secured the mortgage with right of entry to the Surrey property should the debt not be repaid at the appointed date.

Sir Francis Leigh was not only in trouble over his Surrey estates, but by 1692 Charles Sherer demanded the repayment of the mortgages which he held on the Leigh's lands in Shropshire. Leigh was again ordered to repay the mortgage in the Common Dining Hall of the Middle Temple. As he was unable to find the money he was thrust into the debtor's prison, but he was rescued by John Kenrick, who was given power of attorney to obtain the money for Charles Sherer.[6] Sir William Cranmer was now dead and John Kenrick had been made his executor. Thus John Kenrick held in his hands the future of both the Surrey and Shropshire properties, a fact which was of serious consequence to Frances Leigh, the daughter and heir of Sir Francis Leigh.

To return to Sir Francis Leigh. In 1695 he was in trouble again. He had been a member of the Inner Temple, but by this date he appears to have transferred to the Middle Temple. Here he was to share a room with 'Mr. Garfoote', a watchmaker. The room was to be partitioned on the orders of the Treasurer and the Masters of the Bench. Leigh objected and, in the middle of the night, broke down the partition. He was ordered to appear before the Benchers, which he did; he apologised and had the partition replaced. 'Soon after, in a riotous manner, with others, he broke down the partition which he had set up, endangering his own and Garfoote's lives'. The Lord Chief Justice sent his tipstaff to apprehend him, but he was not to be found and was, therefore, expelled from the Middle Temple.[7]

Leigh was not yet at the end of his misfortunes. By 1705 he was imprisoned for debt in Newgate, although 'a Prisoner at large .... and frequently abroad in the Streets of London and in the Country and followed his Business as an Attorney or Solicitor'.[8] Worse was to follow, for in 1705 John Kenrick entered into Sir Francis Leigh's Shropshire estates in right of the unredeemed mortgage which he had taken over from Charles Sherer. In 1711 he took possession of the Surrey property in virtue of his position as executor for Sir William Cranmer.[9] Thus Sir Francis had lost all.

'Some time in July 1710, the said Francis Leigh died, a Prisoner for Debt in Newgate' having left his affairs in the 'utmost Disorder and Confusion' and his daughter and heir 'destitute of any Provision or Means of Subsistence'. She therefore became, at 12 years of age, dependent on the 'Charity and Assistance of her Relations', until she married Jasper Jones in October 1723.[10]

This colourful lord of the manors of Puttenham was an adventurer with no interest in his estates except as a means to raise money and so, perhaps, to enable him to pursue gambling ventures. His successors, as we shall see, may have been a little less unruly, but were quite as much involved in complicated transactions, backed by their manorial estates. Only Lydia Leigh, the mother of Sir Francis, who outlived him, appears to have realised her responsibilities during these troublous times. She remained in Puttenham living, probably, at Shoelands, as she was assessed for her own lands at 'Shoelands Park' at £108.[11] She acted as lord of the manor, in the absence of her son and held View of Frankpledge in 1691. She died in 1711 and was buried in Puttenham.[12]

On the death of her father, Frances Leigh became the lord of the manors of Puttenham in name only, as she was left without money or estate.[13] John Kenrick held the Surrey and Shropshire property; in fact, he held his courts in Puttenham in 1717. It was in order to regain these lands that she and her husband, Jasper Jones, whom she had married in 1723, filed a suit in the Court of Chancery against John Kenrick. The case dragged on for four years. On 13 February 1727 it reached the Bar of the House of Lords when a Judgement by Agreement was given whereby Jasper and Frances Jones were to pay £1,150 to the Respondent John Kenrick, who was to reconvey and reassign the Surrey and Shropshire properties.[14]

This end to the litigation regarding the lands must have been a great relief to the Joneses as they stated in their case that the disputed estates 'are the chief, if not the only Dependence the Appellants have for the support and subsistence of them and their Family'.[15] It is evident that Jasper Jones discharged the debt and regained his wife's lands in Surrey and Shropshire as he held his courts as lord of the manors of Puttenham in 1729[16] and later used these properties to obtain mortgages for himself.

Jasper Jones was a native of Shrewsbury and may have been a

maltster. He probably had small means, hence his plea for the return of the lands in order that he could maintain his family. For 15 years the Joneses appear to have lived in Puttenham and five of their children are entered in the baptismal register of the church there. During this time—from 1729 to 1744—they were beset by money difficulties. This is not to be wondered at as the case which regained for them their property must have brought them nearly to bankruptcy. The amount of research shown in the Appellants case and the time taken in procedure through the courts from 1723 to 1727 would have been extremely costly. They employed Charles Talbot and Thomas Lutwyche as counsel, both of them eminent lawyers, whose fees must have been almost prohibitive for the Joneses. Talbot was Solicitor General at the time and later became Lord Chancellor[17] and Lutwyche[18] was Treasurer of the Inner Temple and recognized as an 'able lawyer'. Added to all these legal expenses the Joneses had to pay Kenrick £1,150 to clear the debts of Sir Francis Leigh and recover the inheritance of Frances Jones. Numerous mortages, covenants and bonds are evidence of Jasper Jones's desperate efforts to keep his head above the rising waters. Like his father-in-law, he was ordered to repay certain sums in the Common Dining Hall of the Inner Temple,[19] but he was no more able to do so than was Sir Francis Leigh.

By 1744 the unequal struggle seems to have been too much for Jasper Jones and he and his wife decided to sell the Puttenham property. It was bought by James Oglethorpe of Westbrook, Godalming, for £4,400. From this sum Jasper and Frances were able to clear the mortgages and retain for themselves £1,038 3s. However, Jasper Jones added to this sum £1,200, which Oglethorpe was ordered to pay for 'quit claims and remises', by the Court of Chancery, before he could obtain release of the property.[20] In 1745 Jasper Jones left his wife in England and departed for Jamaica, where he died 'before 1748'.

From the will which is lodged in the Island Record Office in Jamaica, dated 26 February 1747, we learn that Jasper Jones had taken three of his children with him, namely Frances, John and Mary, and that he appointed his eldest daughter, Frances, as his executrix. He bequeathed 'one half part of all the cargo of goods I brought from England all the proffits ariseing from the sale thereof ... to be equally divided between my three children here now with me Frances, John and Mary and as to the other part of my cargo ... I give ... to my dear and loving wife Frances Jones now in England ... my other affairs in that Kingdom being all settled'.[21] Why Jasper Jones left England and his wife does not appear, nor what the cargo was which he took with him. One point, however, is clear—his affairs in England had all been settled. This probably refers to his debts. For over 150 years the Leighs had kept an insecure hold on the manors of Puttenham, but they now fade into oblivion. We have no knowledge of what happened to seven of the Jones' ten children; we can only watch the Puttenham estates still being tossed about in the financial transactions of its various future lords of the manor.

In 1745 General James Edward Oglethorpe bought from Jasper Jones the manors of Puttenham Priory and Puttenham Bury with the lands in Bramley, Elstead, Tongham and Compton. Oglethorpe was the lord of the manor of Westbrook in Godalming. He was Member of Parliament for Haslemere and was interested in philanthropic work. In this connection he set sail for America in 1732 with 120 men, women and children and founded the colony of Georgia. On his return to England he took up an army career, was involved in crushing the Jacobite invasion of 1745 and in 1744 married an Essex heiress.[22]

Oglethorpe was an interesting person. As well as being a philanthropist, a Member of Parliament, a soldier, he was also a man of letters. He was a friend of Samuel Johnson and moved in his circle. Boswell, in his Life of Samuel Johnson, refers many times to dining with Oglethorpe and meeting at Oglethorpe's house Oliver Goldsmith, Samuel Johnson, Sir Joshua Reynolds, Dr. Campbell amongst others. Boswell speaks of him as having had for 'so long a celebrated name at home and abroad'[23] and of having 'uncommon vivacity of mind and variety of knowledge'.[24] One day, when discussing duelling with Goldsmith and Johnson, Oglethorpe asserted that in all cases of insult it is the aggressor who will be condemned, so it is not necessary for him 'who is affronted' 'to demand a duel'. He then told a story of when he was a young man and was sitting at a table with Prince Eugene of Savoy, the Prince took up a glass of wine and flicked a little in Oglethorpe's face. Oglethorpe paused for a moment and then said 'That's a good joke, but we do it much better in England'. With this remark he flung a glassful of wine in the Prince's face. An old general sitting near by said 'Il a bien fait, mon Prince, vous l'avez

The Priory, Puttenham

commencé'. And 'thus all ended in good humour'.[25] This was the General James Oglethorpe who bought 'the mansion house' (i.e. the Priory) and the lordships of the manors, but who never lived in Puttenham.

The question arises—why did he buy this property for £4,400, since there is no evidence that he ever lived there or intended to do so? He had spent a great deal of his personal fortune on his Georgia venture and had heavily mortgaged his Westbrook estate for that enterprise. The same story applies to Puttenham; from the moment that he obtained completion of his purchase of the manors of Puttenham they appear once more in the mortgage market; he obtained a mortgage of £2,500 on the property and paid an annual interest of £125 on the principle. He must have redeemed the manors later since, in 1757, he mortgaged them once more to Dame Elizabeth Sambrooke for £5,796; but in 1761 Thomas Parker bought the estate and paid Dame Elizabeth Sambrooke, the morgagee, £5,200.[26] It is obvious that James Oglethorpe had had no intention of living in Puttenham. He had settled at Cranham in Essex and had bought the manors of Puttenham as an investment. These lords of the manor, who seem to have lived in a whirl of mortgages, are typical of the age when real estate was the main channel for investment and when landowners and yeomen farmers entered into mortgages, both as mortgagees and mortgagors; banking was not widespread as it is today and only by a system of mortgages could capital be obtained, until such time as bank loans or overdrafts became common.

When we come to Thomas Parker, the next lord of the manor, we find that he took a twofold interest in his property. He used it to obtain mortgages, but also he made the Priory House into a place of gracious living and the surrounding land into a park. Thomas Parker was a member of the Inner Temple and, therefore, conversant with all the intricacies of mortgages; and he used his knowledge to play battledore and shuttle-cock with his Puttenham estates. In 1761 he bought the manors and the 'mansion house' and set about making a country seat for himself, adding to his possessions in Compton, Elstead and Tongham such further lands and tenements as he could secure in Puttenham. The Priory House, when he bought it, was a three-storied building in bargate stone with gables of brick. Parker converted it into a large square mansion with columns, a pediment and a front entrance with a wide 'perron' of steps in the Palladian style. He then landscaped a park of 54 acres and planted it with trees. To enhance his prestige further he obtained permission from the rector and churchwardens to restore the Lady Chapel in the church, which was in a ruinous condition after the fire of 1735. He replaced the east window of the Lady Chapel with a door to form a private entrance for himself. He built a mausoleum under the floor, disturbing the graves of the Lusshers and Wyatts in so doing and set up a large family pew in what was now to be called the 'manorial chapel'.

Parker then turned his attention to his second object—that of acquiring property in the village. In 1765 he bought the malthouse barns and messuage from John Tice. The latter had succeeded to a mortgage on his father's property of over 70 years' standing and evidently he now felt the burden too great. In 1766 Parker bought another malthouse with buildings from John Wood and Mary his wife. In 1768 he bought from Edward Keen a cottage on the south side of the Street and, also, a house and smithy on the same side of it (this property was that which was occupied by Hook in the 1870s and where the butcher's shop was in the 1960s). In the same year John Boxall sold him land at Cutt Mill. In 1771 he obtained from John Tice 'land, messuage and buildings' in Puttenham Street and from Edward Keen lands up Lascombe Lane. Parker was certainly determined to be the most important landowner in the village. He does not, however, appear to have been a kindly man, as an indenture shows that he and one, Masterman, drew up an agreement whereby Thomas Parker deprived his wife of her dower in connection with the Priory.[27] His tomb in Seale churchyard describes him as First Provincial Grand Master of the Surrey Branch of the Freemasons.

If Thomas Parker was not a property speculator, he obviously had some of the instincts of one. In 1766 he bought Hampton, in Seale, converted the house on classical lines and began the chain of lakes which separate Puttenham from Seale. In 1775 he put up the Priory property for sale, but retained the manorial rights of the Puttenham manors. These were bought by Nathaniel Snell when he purchased Hampton in 1792 and were exercised by later owners of Hampton. They were returned to Puttenham, as a result of the efforts of Mark Smallpeice in 1888.[28] In 1775 the Priory estate was put up for sale by Thomas Parker and the house was described by the auctioneers, Messrs. Langford of Covent Garden, as 'a residence devoutly to be wished' because of the 'acknowledged salubrity of air, pureness of water, politeness of environ'. This was to be sold 'together with the pews in the Chancel (lately beautified)'.[29] The property was bought by Admiral Cornish, but Thomas Parker lived at Hampton until he died in 1791 leaving an estate worth £193! Presumably all his Seale property was mortgaged. He was buried in Seale churchyard. With Admiral Cornish a new type of owner of the Priory estate appears—no longer are they connected with the Inns of Court, nor were they fighting desperately to keep their heads above the waters of financial ruin by mortgages and counter mortgages. The insecurity of the 18th century had passed and had been replaced by the security and decorum of the 19th century.

Francis Leigh, Jasper Jones, General Oglethorpe and Thomas Parker are all colourful people with few of the characteristics we would now expect from the lord of a manor. Their interests appear to have been dictated by the possibility of financial gain or merely of getting rid of their many mortgages. To us today this seems almost an amoral obsession, but it was typical of the times and not only did the gentry engage in this kind of transaction, but it was practised by some of the villagers. In the Inns of Court this traffic in mortgages was a very common practice among the gentry and was often carried out in the common dining halls and was even undertaken by members on behalf of other members. Mortgages were of the utmost importance to the yeoman farmer and even the artisan, as the indentures in the hands of the Puttenham History Society show. It appears that they used mortgages as frequently as we today obtain bank loans—for buying new stock, improving the land and erecting new buildings. Caleb Woods mortgaged his malthouse and buildings and so did Edward Keen. The Revd. Thomas Swift mortgaged the trees on his church property, and John Tice took out a mortgage on his farm in order to build a malthouse. This sytem, which seems precarious to us, was in fact the only way in which any farmer could obtain capital for expansion. The banking system, as we know it, was in its infancy in the 17th and 18th centuries. The banks do not appear to have been employed in any way by the lords of the manor or by their tenants.

NOTES

1. Woods MSS. Godalming Hundred, vol.17, p.194.
2. Ibid., p.212^{S}.
3. *Journals of the House of Lords,* vol.xxiii (1726-1731), p.184.
4. Browns Reports, *House of Lords Parliamentary Cases,* 1727, p.244. For further details of this case, see below n.8.
5. Indentures in the possession of the Puttenham and Wanborough History Society.
6. From Indentures and an article on Francis Leigh by A.E. Drake-Brockman in 'Papers read to the Puttenham and Wanborough History Society', 1967-8.
7. *Middle Temple Records,* vol.iii, 1650-1703, p.1436, referring to the year 1695.
8. The Respondent's Case, p.4 in *House of Lords Appeal Cases 1725-1727,* House of Lords Library. The case is printed in *The English Reports,* vol.ii: *House of Lords,* London 1901 (reprinted from 5 Brown P.C. Case 14), pp.665-661. Photostat copies of the Appellants' Case and the Respondent's Case are in the Shrewsbury Record Office (SRO 1007/1).
9. Ibid.
10. Ibid.
11. E.W. Brayley, *A History of the County of Surrey,* London 1841, vol.v, p.240.
12. G.B. Gosling, 'Notes on the History of Puttenham', fol.6.
13. The Appellants' Case, op. cit.
14. *Journals of the House of Lords,* vol.xxiii (1726-1731), p.184.
15. The Appellants' Case, op. cit.
16. G.B. Gosling, 'Notes on the History of Puttenham' fol.6.
17. *Dictionary of National Biography,* vol.lv, p.306.
18. Ibid., vol.xxxiv, p.302.
19. Indenture in the possession of the Puttenham and Wanborough History Society.
20. Ibid.
21. Will of Jasper Jones, entered 25 February 1747 in the Island Record Office in Jamaica (Ref. 686/69), certified by Janette

J. Dixon under the seal of the Record Office at Spanish Town, Jamaica, West Indies, 1 July 1970, in the possession of the Puttenham and Wanborough History Society.

22. *Dictionary of National Biography,* vol.xlii, p.47.
23. James Boswell, *Life of Samuel Johnson* ed. Roger Inkpen, London 1970, vol.i, p.519.
24. Ibid., vol.ii, p.636.
25. Ibid., vol.i, pp.409-410.
26. Indentures in the possession of the Puttenham and Wanborough History Society.
27. Indentures in the possession of the Puttenham and Wanborough History Society.
28. Ibid.
29. Particulars of Sale in Guildford Muniment Room. 85/2/1(1) No.4.

VIII

CHURCH AND VILLAGE IN THE EIGHTEENTH CENTURY

CHURCHWARDENS' ACCOUNTS are a most useful source for the history of both church and parish, since the duties of these men were so multifarious. Copies of the Churchwardens' Accounts of Puttenham exist from 1718 and they enable us to piece together, in some small measure, the life of the village in the 18th century, which, except for a disastrous fire at the church in 1735, can have differed little from any other small English village in the South-east of the country. Other documents, articles and books can also be of help, such as taxation returns, the remarks of the Revd. Thomas Swift and the description of Puttenham in Aubrey's *Surrey*.

Before turning to the Churchwardens' accounts let us see how these other sources can help to build up a picture of the village. In 1664 a new tax was imposed on the hearths in houses possessing more than one hearth. The returns show that 18 houses in Puttenham had one hearth and so were exempt, but 37 houses had two or more. This emphasizes two points—one that the number of sizeable houses had increased since the late 16th century, when one-hearth houses were in the majority and, secondly, that, by reckoning five in each family and the number of houses to be 55, the population would be about 275—one third of the number today. This village of 275 inhabitants is described by Aubrey as lying 'upon a fine gravel, and on an ascent from whence is a good prospect of the country and is remarkable for its situation, the wholeness of its most beneficial air and other desirable advantages to render life easy and pleasant'. The rector at the turn of the century, the Revd. Thomas Swift, further expatiates on the desirability of Puttenham—'ye situation of this place is so healthy as to deserve a Remark as ye finest stroke of your Learned Pen can give it, such is ye salubrity of its air as did thos wealthy Citizens know who want nothing so much as Health, I might say ... yt they would come & make a City here'.[1] Mercifully no city was built here and the population had only risen to 361 in 1801. This, then, is the village which will be seen through the accounts of the churchwardens and which was hoping for peace after the troublous times of the Civil War. Probably it was peaceful until 16 April 1735. However, the Churchwardens must tell us of the life of Puttenham before we reach that date.

Churchwardens were elected by the Vestry, a meeting at which all ratepayers could attend. Those elected to the office had to appear at the visitation of the Ordinary to be sworn in. From that moment their duties were legion. They had to make presentments at the archdeacon's court; look after the church fabric, except for the chancel which was the rector's responsibility; supervise the choir and visiting preachers who were strangers; keep an eye on the bell-ringers; prevent undesirable people from entering the church; keep down vermin; provide the church with bread and wine and be ready to deal with 'any other business'. Parish assistance appears many times in the accounts, not only for those in the village, but for those in transit. Probably travellers from Guildford to the West were thankful for a little help as they plodded their way through the village. John Marsh, churchwarden in 1723, noted 'to a woman in travell and to Elizabeth Smith for trouble at her (confinement), 2s. 6d.'; 'gave to a big belied woman, 1s. 6d.'; 'given to sum seamen y had been captives in Turkey, 6d.'; 'carrying vagrants through ye county'. Whenever the constable was needed he had to be paid by the churchwardens, e.g., 'paid George Avenell for constable's charges for carrying Rogues to goal—£1 3s. 6d.'. A tragic entry appears when William Tice was churchwarden in 1719—'Paid the charges for going to London after William Swift, paid the hire of 2 horses, 10s. Paid the charges of William Marshall when we went after William Swift.' William Swift was probably the n'er-do-well son of the rector, Thomas Swift, who, it was said, ran away from an apprenticeship, perhaps in Puttenham, as he later appeared on the parish list of paupers. Eventually, he may have been executed for highway robbery. Charles Kerry refers to this, but he cannot substantiate the statement. We now find the churchwardens concerned in more mundane matters, 'paid for a cover for ye town well'; 'for a brock's [badger's] head, 1s.'; 'for 6 foxes heads, 6s.'; 'for a pair of stockins for Will Swift'—he would be given these as a pauper. Bells and bell-ringing were also the province of the churchwardens and, in the 18th century, as today, bell-ringing was both an art and a pastime. To this the churchwardens gave most careful attention; indeed, payment of bell-ringers, new bells and new bell ropes, were their responsibility. In 1718 William Tice has this entry—'the churchwardens and the Parish of Puttenham' agreed to a mortgage of church lands towards 'the use of newe casting 4 bells into five'. In 1735, 'that at the meeting aforesaid it was agreed that "five shillings should be allowed out of the Parish Rate to the Ringers on Easter Monday instead of a Breakfast" '. The change in churchmanship from the early 16th century is apparent in the Accounts, where the Word, as opposed to the Sacrament, is emphasized. For instance, extra accommodation for seating was needed when long sermons became the vogue and standing through them would be tedious, and in Puttenham, as in many other villages, a gallery was built at the west end of the church. The entry runs '1721 Paid to Thomas Tice towards ye gallery, £1 18s. 8d.'. Again, to give the pulpit more importance in the churches larger ones were being built and here Puttenham followed the fashion, in 1727 the churchwardens paid for a new pulpit. The bread and wine for communion had to be provided by the churchwardens. George Smith, churchwarden 1755, did his best to make a correct entry when he wrote 'for bread and wind *[sic]* for Christmas 5s.'.[2]

These extracts from the Churchwardens' Accounts in the 18th century give some small picture of the village at that time. They show the attempt which was made to keep law and order, to give public assistance, to encourage the art of bell-ringing, to provide the correct fittings for the church, such as the pulpit and gallery, to meet the churchmanship of the times and to keep down vermin in the village—a breathless medley of commitments. However, the resources of certain churchwardens were going to be taxed to the uttermost in 1735 and afterwards.

On the morning of 16 April 1735, a strong South-east wind was blowing. Suddenly a cry of 'Fire' was raised in the Street. The blacksmith's shop, south west of the church, was on fire. The fire spread to the cottages higher up the hill, reached the church, caught the steeple, melted the bells, burnt part of the nave roof, badly damaged the north aisle and even caused some destruction in the Lady Chapel. The only water available was from the 'town well', but the villagers worked hard and eventually the fire was extinguished; yet considerable damage had been done. However, Ralph Toft, the acting Churchwarden, immediately took action. He organized an appeal for help from other churches by means of briefs. A brief was an appeal to incumbents and churchwardens of other churches for assistance. Usually a brief was read from the pulpit and contributions were taken at the church door. It was customary to send out a large number of these briefs, but there is no record as to how many were sent from Puttenham in 1735. Toft's Churchwardens Accounts show only two responses—one from St. Clement's, Eastcheap, of £2 2s. 6d. and the other, either from St. Martin's, Orgar, a benefice united with St. Clement's, or from St. Martin's, Ongar, in Essex, the gift of 13s. The writing is not very legible and it is difficult to state categorically which church contributed the 13s. The important fact was that Toft secured some help, if small, towards rebuilding. This system of briefs was the only means of obtaining financial help in times of disaster, when insurance was hardly known. Immediately after the fire Toft had ordered the parish clerk, Richard Bezar, and his wife, Jessie, to remove the seats from the church and to clear the charred debris. The legend goes that Jessie complained that this was a thirsty job and that, accordingly, Toft ordered Bezar to be supplied with '3s. for beer'. Goodman Strudwick, the publican, was also ordered to supply beer to the amount of 6s. 6d. 'for ye men y extinguished ye fire at ye church'.[3] However, Toft's work was not done, for the Accounts reveal five years of effort to restore the church. The entries are many, including 6d. to 'Tho. Welland' for writing the articles between 'ye parish and ye workmen'; '1s. for letting ye ceiling of the church'; '50 bushels of lime for mortar for the porch'; 'Pd. ye bill to Wm. Tice for ye Pullpit £6 10s. 0d.'. The metal from the bells was sent to the foundry to be re-cast and Toft spent 2s. 7½d. 'for meeting ye gentlemen about ye bells' in Guildford.[4] Eventually the restoration was completed, except for the Lady Chapel. There was obviously not sufficient money to meet the cost of this, and it had to wait 20 years until Thomas Parker drove his bargain with the rector and churchwardens in 1761 and rebuilt it as a manorial chapel.

The incumbent of the parish at the time of the fire was the

Revd. Thomas Swift, who held the living from 1694 until his death at the age of 86 in 1752. During more than half a century he took the services in Puttenham church, Sunday after Sunday with little respite, and it is with compassion that we view his life. He, like many of the clergy in country parishes during the 17th and 18th centuries, must have felt frustrated and isolated as the years went by, until he became embittered and without hope. Many of these parish priests were members of county families or had been brought up in a world of letters at Oxford or Cambridge. After ordination they accepted country livings and, in those days of poor communications, were cut off from any intellectual pursuits and were very often condemned to a life of near poverty.

Thomas Swift was a cousin of Sir William Temple and was related to Dean Swift. Thomas went to Balliol College, Oxford, and obviously lived within an intellectual society. It is a matter of controversy as to whether he may have been the author of *A Tale of a Tub*. However, this is unlikely and it is probable that his only publication was a sermon. He went to Puttenham as a young man, perhaps not yet priested, and lived for the rest of his 58 years as rector there. Martha, his first wife, presented him with ten children, but she died giving birth to the tenth, and the deaths of the children seem to follow their births in rapid succession, according to the church register. The eldest, William, appears to have been of little credit to the family, since, as we have seen, he was brought back from London at the charge of the parish.

In 1730 Thomas married as his second wife Ann, of Malton in Yorkshire, in Puttenham church.[5] There is no indication as to who she was, but Swift was obviously anxious to do his best for her, perhaps to compensate her for taking on the problems of his large family. In 1747 he took out a mortgage for 2½ acres of land in Shamley Green, which he left her in his will and with it sufficient money to redeem the mortgage.[6] Another indenture in the possession of the Puttenham and Wanborough History Society deals with a release to her of lands in Puttenham, so it is probable that she was not left entirely penniless, when she had to leave the rectory on her husband's death. Swift seems not to have found it easy to raise the money to provide for his wife, since, in 1749, he mortgaged his trees on his glebe land to one, John Marsh.[7] Later, Ann followed her husband's example and raised a mortgage on some land with Thomas Parker,[8] as she was obviously in need of ready cash. In following this practice of taking out mortgages Thomas and Ann Swift were only pursuing the example of their contemporaries.

In 1705 Thomas Swift had to reply to some enquiries about the condition of the parish of Puttenham. The answers were short and not very helpful; in fact, they show an attitude of complete indifference–perhaps the iron was already entering his soul. To the question 'What part of the Tithes is your church or chapel endowed with'? he replied in one word 'All'. Other questions asked were 'If your church or chapel was founded since the reformation, when and by whom'? And 'What library is settled or settling in your Parish and by whom'? Or 'If the yearly value of your rectory, vicarage or chapelry be under £30, how much'?[9] To all of these the laconic reply was 'No'. A report on Puttenham by the bishop of Winchester after a visitation in 1725 perhaps helps us to understand the feeling of desolation which Swift experienced. It runs 'No chapel, no lecturer, no curate, no Papist, one Quaker, no gentleman, nor any school but what teaches children to read and write'.[10] Nevertheless, as we have seen, Swift was eloquent on the countryside of Puttenham.

In 1738 Swift became involved in a long and complicated law-suit, known as 'H. Wyatt *v.* P. Wyatt and Thos. Swift'. During these proceedings reference is made to the boarding school kept by him in Puttenham.[11] Whether this was the school 'what teaches children to read and write' is not clear, but if, as the visitation report says, there was no school except this one, it does not look as though Swift's school was of a high standard. Thomas Swift died in May 1752 and was buried in Puttenham churchyard, where his first wife and numerous children had been laid before him. It is difficult to think of him as anything other than a saddened and disappointed man. His domestic life for the first 14 years was, surely, a continual round of children being born and children dying and he must have been cut off from all intellectual interests. Sadly, however, we must realise that Thomas Swift was typical of many country parsons in the 18th century.

Swift did not live to see the restoration of the church completed after the fire of 1735, nor do we know whether he accepted the type of churchmanship which it expressed and which is pictured for us in the Hassell drawings now in the church. The small altar and the large pulpit depicted illustrate the emphasis on the preaching of the Word rather than the Sacrament in this period. No cross appears on the altar, but the Ten Commandments and the Royal Arms are prominently displayed; a gallery is shown at the west end where the village instrumentalists played the accompaniment to the metrical psalms of Tate and Brady; the font is placed in the chancel and seems to take on the same insignificant appearance as the altar. Only on Sacrament Sunday, four times yearly, did the chancel play any part in the church services, mattins and evensong being conducted from the nave. Any picture of the interior of a church in the 18th and early 19th centuries would illustrate the changes in theological thought which had come about since the Reformation and Hassell shows that Puttenham was a typical example of the ecclesiology of the period.

By now Puttenham, with other villages in West Surrey, was beginning to take on the appearance of gentle prosperity. There was a new stimulus to farming throughout the county and agricultural communities on the greensand were not slow to take advantage of it. The yield from crops had increased rapidly and larger barns for storage were built in many stackyards. Puttenham was no exception. There are a considerable number of 17th-century barns still standing in the village today; these barns were looked upon as very valuable possessions and are often mentioned in the wills of the farmers. Hop growing had also developed in this area and in September the villages were alive with hop pickers preparing the crop to be sent to Weyhill or to Farnham for the hop market. By the end of the century hop kilns were built in many of the villages, as they were in Puttenham, where one was in use until 1970.

In this new world of farming fresh names appear among the yeomen farmers of Puttenham and some of them are found to be occupying the larger houses. Francis Simmonds (1700-65) is referred to as a yeoman and tenant farmer living at Shoelands. He was obviously a man of some account, as we find him along with Toft as one of the churchwardens in 1743, coping successfully with the aftermath of the fire at the church. His son bought Shoelands in 1767 from its owner, Giles Strangeway. Thomas Selwyn rented Rodsall from Richard Wyatt and John Marsh was tenant at Frollebury (Frosbury). Another family, the Fludders, are often referred to throughout the 18th century as yeomen and

The village inn

were obviously men of ability, holding office as churchwardens, way-wardens or overseers of the poor. They lived in the farm house in Hook Lane, which is now two cottages known as Hook Lane Cottages. In the next century the Fludders are still yeomen, but live in Street Farm. Another interesting person is Caleb Woods, son of Caleb Woods, the Quaker, who was fined for failing to take the oath of Ale-taster at Guildford. Father and son were maltsters in Puttenham and were largely instrumental in building the Friends Meeting House in Godalming. They owned a malt-house, barns, farm buildings, gate rooms and about three acres of land in the Street. These premises were left to the younger Caleb's daughter and she mortgaged them for £100 in 1748, but for what purpose does not appear. Caleb Wood, father and son were obviously men of substance and important persons in the Quaker world of Godalming and Surrey.[12]

The wills of the period are interesting as some of them refer to the lesser known yeomen and they indicate the preoccupation of the village with arable farming. In 1702 William Tice left to his son 'the lower end of the Barn with free egress and regress to the said Barn and Pond'.[13] In 1717 John Tice left this property to his brother 'with free egress and regress to the Barn and the Pond for water'.[14] In 1734 William Snelling, yeoman, left '1 messuage, 1 Barn, 15 acres arable' to Francis Simmonds. In 1766 Abraham Toft, yeoman, left to his daughter '100 roods ... near the Publick House bearing the sign of the Queen's Head ... and the new erected tenement bearing the sign of the Jolly Farmer'.[15] This is the first mention of two more public houses in Puttenham. Further information which we gain from wills shows that, although the farmer wanted a more commodious house, he had little idea of comfort in furnishings. In one will reference is made to two stools and a chair in the hall; a bed, four holland sheets, coverlette and chest in the bedroom; two brass pots, kettle and spit in the kitchen and some pewter. Robert Clifton, yeoman, left tables, stools, chest, four beds, two changes of clothes 'which were of little worth'. A Wyatt will appears as rather a human document: he leaves to 'Grandfather Peter Courthorpe Esquire and my grandmother his wife 40s. apiece. All my Uncles and Aunts 20d. apiece. Aunt Frances wife of Uncle Burrell 10s.'.[16] It is interesting to speculate about the kind of life which these yeomen lived.

Village life in the 18th century was largely uneventful and

parochial. The villagers themselves were simple and were generally unlettered; even some of the churchwardens were unable to sign their names and had to make their mark at the end of the accounts. From the church registers it is possible to distinguish a few of the village artisans. We read of Balchin, the shoemaker, Litzenburg the publican; and Litzenburg, the stone-mason, Saunders and Wyatt, also shoemakers at different times in the century, Tice and Stovold, carpenters; two village nurses, Dame Coles and Dame Green, who seem to have been without any professional ability and were commonly called 'Old Sharks'; and one village schoolmaster, George Eastmond, who, it is said, held office for 12 years.

Belief in fairies and old wives tales, fantasies and spells came into the lives of these villagers. Stories of fairies, or 'Pharisees' as they were called in this part of Surrey, were firmly believed in and were passed down from generation to generation. Charles Kerry has recorded some of them for us. Let us listen to Kerry and some of his parishioners talking together outside the *Jolly Farmer,* where Kerry found them sitting on the bench in the sun. Kerry was dressed in the frock coat, flat hat and boots which were worn by the clergy a century ago. Cranham, Durbridge and Alexander were in their working smocks and Steer was in the loose shirt and knee breeches of an innkeeper. Kerry had just declared that there were no such things as fairies. He was talking to old Cranham, who was 80 and had been a carter to Farmer Hewett; to Durbridge, who was Allden's ploughman, and to Alexander the grave-digger—all of whom could remember the tales of the 18th century told them by their fathers. As they were talking, Steer, the innkeeper, came out and joined them. Cranham declared that he firmly believed in fairies and that his father had done so too. 'Some fairies are good fairies and some are bad', he said. 'The bad ones would steal horses from the stables and ride over the fields on hurdles'. 'These be Pharisees', said old Cranham, 'that is what we call the bad fairies. They would take the best horse out of a farmer's stable and ride it till it was almost spent, then they would return it to the stable and forget to rub it down, so when the carter came in the morning he would find his horse wet and shivering'. 'Now, sir,' said Cranham, 'there was only one remedy and that was certain—hang a horse-shoe over the keyhole of the stable, for no fairy will go through a horse-shoe.' 'I will tell you a story about Pharisees, which is gospel true', said Durbridge. 'As I was coming down Dark Lane from Shoelands one winter evening, I was overtaken by creatures on hurdles, travelling at such a rate that the wind from their flight flung me into a hole in the road and there I lay panting'. 'My father told me', broke in old Cranham, 'that the good fairies would help when you was desperate to get in the harvest.' 'Often', he said, 'they would work at night cutting the corn and leave it ready for gathering in the morning'. Then Alexander, the grave-digger, joined in in support of old Cranham's belief in the supernatural. 'My wife', said he, 'was ill and I knewed it was because of witchcraft, so I got a pigeon's heart, stuffed it with pins, baked it and put it beside her, she soon recovered. This, sir', he insisted, 'was far better than Dr. Balchin's pills'. Steer said nothing, but he nodded his head in approval at his customers' tales.

It was not only the men who had these tales to tell. The women talked to Kerry when he was visiting his parishioners. Old Mother Brown, who did the neighbours' washing, advised him on how to sit a goose. 'Always place it on its eggs with its head to the South and its tail to the North', she said; 'if you don't do this not an egg will hatch'. Mrs. Brown was quite definite about this. Mrs. Pierce from Gatwick had another housewife's tale. She warned Kerry 'Never leave your hearth dirty when you go to bed at night, if you do, the fairies will come upstairs and pinch you black and blue'. Whether Kerry took this advice to heart and passed it on to his landlady, we do not know. One more story came from Mrs. Pierce. 'When I was a young woman', she said, 'we always pierced a wax candle with pins to bring our young men to see us'. All these stories and many others are given by Kerry in his records written between 1868 and 1874. He tells us that they had been repeated from generation to generation and were still believed implicitly.

We learn of quaint customs and amusements in the village through the antiquarian curiosity of Charles Kerry. He tells of 'Gooding on St. Thomas' Day'. This 'Gooding' was a way by which the poor women could get materials for their Christmas fare. Wearing red cloaks and with hoods over their bonnets these poor women visited the houses of the wealthier inhabitants and were given 'goodings', which consisted of some kind of provisions. Daniel Simmonds gave them rye, which was ground free of charge by Hale, the miller, at Cutt Mill. The flour could then be used for making Christmas cakes. Others gave different ingredients for the cakes, such as fat and dried fruit. Watching on St. John's Eve was another, rather morbid, custom. A certain number of the villagers would sit up all night in the church porch and if they fasted and did not fall asleep they felt sure they would see passing before them those who were to die during the year.

For the men a more healthy amusement offered—this was Morris Dancing. At the end of the 18th century this was a favourite pastime and Puttenham was famous locally for the skill of its dancers. Furlanger, the carter, wore bells on his legs and ankles and was always loudly cheered as he danced down the Street. On one occasion he and two of his friends took a load of carrots to London. At the house where they stayed the night there was a Morris Dancing competition and Cranham won the prize. Apparently Furlanger was the only dancer who wore the bells and when he died this picturesque custom was dropped.

Excitement came into the lives of most of the villagers at the end of the 18th century through the increase of smuggling and the means by which many of them could participate in a small way. There are probably few villages in South-east England which have not tales to tell of smuggling. A great many of these can be taken with a pinch of salt, but Rodsall, Puttenham and Seale were on the direct route to Bagshot Heath, which is known to have been a rendezvous for smugglers. The yeomen farmers in these villages appear to have taken advantage of the chance of obtaining spirits from the smugglers as they passed on their way North from the Sussex coast. Robert Keen would always leave food for men and horses in his field at Rodsall, called Puckstool Bottom, and would find contraband left in return. The cottage at Monks Grove is said to have been a hiding place for spirits. According to Kerry, the occupant, William Goddard, made a double floor in a bedroom and hid smuggled goods in the cavity, covering the loose boards with a large double bed. Wells in Puttenham and Seale are said to have been hiding places; they were widened just above the water line and contraband was hidden there. Birkbeck, the farmer at Wanborough farm, was supposed to have met smugglers by night on the Heath to obtain spirits. Not only did the yeomen take advantage of the smugglers' visits, but so did the other villagers. Often they had to assist in getting the contraband through the village by putting it in the wagons and covering it with hay or

Morris dancing

straw. In return they received their nips of brandy in the fields and their wives were given yellow silk scarves brought from France.[17] These stories of smuggling were related to Kerry by 'old John Cranham' as remembrances of his boyhood at the end of the 18th century. Thus, the men and women of the village told their stories, believed in their fantasies and, perhaps, benefited from the smugglers who passed through Puttenham.

NOTES

1. A letter in the Bodleian Library, Oxford, dated 1st Oct. 1717 (MS. Rawl. D.1194, No.8) quoted by Robert Martin Adams in The Authorship of 'A Tale of a Tub', in *Modern Philology*, vol.64, 1966/67, Appendix C, p.231.
2. From copies of the Accounts of the Churchwardens in the Kerry Documents. The originals have been lost.
3. Kerry, vol.ii, p.105.
4. Ibid., p.106.
5. Robert Martin Adams, loc. cit.
6. Indenture in the possession of the Puttenham and Wanborough History Society.
7. Ibid.
8. Ibid.
9. Surrey Archaeological Collections XII, p.169.
10. *V.C.H., Surrey* vol. iii, p.58.
11. Guildford Muniment Room, 5/6/54.
12. Indenture and will in the possession of the Puttenham and Wanborough History Society.
13. Woods MSS. Collections, vol.4, p.23.
14. Ibid., p.23[a].
15. Ibid., p.38.
16. Woods MSS. Godalming Hundred, vol.17, p.231.
17. Kerry, vol.vi, pp.129, 130, 140.

IX

PAROCHIAL ADMINISTRATION I
THE POOR LAW

THE PATTERN of parochial administration, which began under the Tudors was nowhere more clearly in evidence than in the working of the Poor Law. Pauperism was a problem which increased in intensity from the time of Elizabeth until the Poor Law Act of 1834. Different methods of dealing with the question were tried during the centuries. Elizabeth's Act of 1601 laid down that each parish was to be responsible for the maintenance of its poor and that Overseers, or Guardians of the Poor were to be appointed to care for those who were penniless. Acts of 1609 and 1610 ordered that Houses of Correction should be built. In 1662 the odious Act of Settlement was passed, which enabled Justices of the Peace to send back to his original place of settlement any stranger who had entered another parish and become a pauper. In 1697 artisans or labourers could only come into a village if certificates were brought from their places of settlement guaranteeing that those parishes would receive them back if they became paupers. This Act led to tragic incidents, as will be seen from some of the Puttenham Settlement Orders.

Further attempts were made to wrestle with the increasing problem of poor relief. In 1781 by Gilbert's Act parishes were allowed to share workhouses and, thereby, expenses. In 1794 Overseers were permitted to give out-door relief instead of consigning all paupers to the workhouse. In the following year the Speenhamland system was adopted in many places, whereby the parish supplemented wages out of rates. In spite of all these attempts to deal with the problem, matters became worse at the beginning of the 19th century and the poor rate soared to unprecedented heights. It was not until 1834 that the Poor Law Amendment Act was passed and the State assumed responsibility for poor relief.

The documents relating to poor law administration in Puttenham[1] show that the village must have closely followed in local administration the pattern envisaged by the State for poor relief. Praiseworthy but inadequate attempts to cope with poverty in the village appear early, in wills already mentioned. Edmund Ede left 'to the poor people 111s.'. George Billinghurst bequeathed 'to the poore of the parysshe church of Puttenham 10s.'. There is no record of immediate reaction to Elizabeth's Act of 1601, but undoubtedly the Vestry would have met, Overseers would have been appointed and a poor rate levied. However, at some time during the 17th century the parish must have built a House of Correction according to the terms of the Acts of 1609 and 1610. By a chance reference in a clerical report it is possible to locate this building. In 1849, John Chandler, rural dean, reported to the Bishop of Winchester that buildings on the glebe land, where the new rectory had been built 'had been occupied by the paupers of the parish' and 'were in a ruinous condition and should be demolished'.[2] It appears that the old workhouse, which was not used after 1790, was situated in the grounds of the present manor house. Hence we can imagine the paupers of the parish living under appalling conditions in the workhouse facing Hook Lane. A workhouse on land which is now a gracious park is somewhat ironical. Nevertheless the Overseers were making an attempt to deal with a terribly difficult situation.

In 1662 the Act of Settlement of Charles II came to the help of the Overseers, although it brought fear and tragedy to the pauper. From the time of this Act sad little expeditions went to Puttenham, or from Puttenham to other villages, bearing paupers and their families from one parish to another until they reached their place of settlement. The place of settlement was named on certificates carried by all workers after 1697. The trouble connected with obtaining this certificate is shown in one addressed to the Overseers of Puttenham from the Overseers of Godalming in 1725, who certify 'that they do own and acknowledge Robert Rowle and Mary his wife to be inhabitants legally settled in ... Godalming and We will receive them in case of Want as the law directs'. The names and seals of two Churchwardens and five Overseers are added. In another certificate from Godalming, dated 1772, the officers recognize 'John, Elizabeth and Mary Budd as inhabitants legally settled in Godalming'. It could not have been easy for the Rowles and the Budds to go through the correct channels to obtain these certificates. We wonder whether the two families found work and happiness in Puttenham. However, it is when we come to removal orders that the cruelty of the system appears.

As soon as a man was unable to support himself or his family the Overseers of the parish in which he was living applied to his place of settlement to receive him and, thereby, they were able to get rid of the family and so save the burden of supporting them from the rates. The Overseers were not cruel, but they were harassed by the increasing number of poor and the rising poor rate. All but one of the Removal Orders connected with Puttenham date from 1820 and will be considered later, but there is one of 1791 sent by the Overseers of Puttenham to their opposite numbers in Elstead demanding the removal of William Legg, his wife and four children to Elstead. This, as were all the others, was signed by the Justices of the Peace. Puttenham was responsible for taking the family to the village boundaries and then it fell to Elstead to remove them to their own workhouses and support them. This was a comparatively easy removal, but others were more difficult and more tragic when long distances were involved.

The Overseers of Puttenham now had their own workhouse, they had a poor rate of 2s. 6d. in the £ in 1793[3] and they had put into working order the policy of settlement; but still the problem was not solved for relief of the poor either in this or any other village. Accordingly, when Gilbert's Act was passed in 1781 allowing unions of workhouses to ease the cost to the villages, Puttenham decided to discuss a possible union with Ash. A meeting was held at the *Jolly Farmer Inn* on 5 March 1790, at which the parish officers agreed, 'persuant to the Directions of an Act of Parliment of the twenty-second year of King George the Third, instituted for the Better Maintenance and Employment of the poor', that £5 p.a. should be added to the poor rate to enable them 'to Except the proposals of the Parish Officers and Inhabitants of the Parish of Puttenham ... and for uniting the two parishes of Ash and Puttenham for the better maintenance and Employment of the poor'.[4] This minute was signed by the Churchwardens, Overseers and other parish officials. Obviously a Vestry Meeting of the ratepayers had been held in the church to discuss the vexed question of poor relief. The possibility of union with Ash had been considered, but no decision had been taken. However, a committee of parish officials was suggested to look into the advantages and disadvantages of the scheme and to meet at a later date to decide what course should be taken. This committee wisely met in the hostelry of the *Jolly Farmer,* where its members would be warm on a March evening and where they could partake of Litzenburg's ale. As a result they agreed that they would join with Ash in sharing the House of Industry in that village. This would be cheaper, which would please the ratepayers and, perhaps, they thought it might be more humanitarian, since better food could be provided for the inmates and closer inspection by the magistrates would lead to improved conditions. Anyhow, one can imagine them concluding that it was impossible to continue with the workhouse at Puttenham, which had to be run on less than the proverbial shoe-string. Thus in 1790 the Union of Ash and Puttenham was formed; by taking this step Puttenham deviated from the general pattern, since Gilbert Unions were in the minority in the country as a whole. W.E. Tate tells us that in 1834 'there were only sixty-seven Gilbert Unions, covering 924 parishes'.[15]

To what were the pauper inhabitants of Puttenham condemned? Let us try to picture life in the House of Industry. Before outdoor relief was allowed in 1794 all paupers (whether unable to work or just unable to find it), their children, the chronically sick, women pregnant with bastards and the mentally ill would be sent to Ash. These unfortunates were taken from Puttenham by the carter detailed for the work. The cart, probably open to the weather, would have bumped along the ill-kept roads, causing suffering to anyone who was ill. The sad little expedition proceeded up Oliver Hill, along the Hog's Back, down the lane into Ash and, bearing right, arrived at the House of Industry. This low stone building with small windows, which still stands, much altered as a private house, held little welcome for the newcomers. On the right of the gateway was a barn, badly lit and faced inside and out with stone, cold and cheerless; this was where the inmates worked long hours with little hope of release. On arrival the paupers would enter the house where, in a square stone-flagged room they would be met by the Master, named Lambard (sometimes spelt Lamble). They would then be detailed to their dormitories, husbands and wives being separated. The food was frugal, consisting largely of gruel and vegetable stews, the sanitary arrangements were unspeakable and medical care was almost nil. During the day everyone would have to work and they would only return to their cold cheerless dormitories at night. Here they would sleep the sleep of exhaustion and awake to another day of despair. The poet George Crabbe writes of a workhouse, perhaps with some exaggeration, but not entirely divorced from the truth:

There children dwell who know no parent's care,
Parents, who know no children's love, dwell there,
Heartbroken matrons on their joyless bed,
Forsaken wives, and mothers never wed.

In the majority of workhouses the master had secured his position by bidding for it. For him it was a commercial proposition; so it was up to him to make what he could out of his mastership. In Farnham, Christophulus Chitty, having made a successful bid for the workhouse, undertook to feed and clothe 45 inmates for 2s. each per week.[1] Probably Ash was run on the same lines. No wonder it was everyone's desperate effort to keep out of the workhouse. When outdoor relief was allowed in 1794, matters were slightly better. Then the able-bodied poor were set to work and were also given help out of the rates; this was distributed by the Overseer in the church. The account entries are headed 'At the Church' and then there follow the amounts given and to whom.

One's sympathy goes out to the Overseers, as well as to the paupers. These officials appear to seize upon every direction by the government, or example of fellow Overseers, which might help them. In 1799 the idea of supplementing wages out of the rates had not been entirely successful, so the Overseers of Puttenham were anxious to try a new expedient—the Speenhamland system, which adapted relief in kind to the size of the family, in addition to monetary relief. Although this system never received Parliamentary sanction it was freely adopted in the South and the Midlands; there are not many references to it in Surrey, but a minute in the Poor Law Account Book seems to indicate that it was accepted in Puttenham. It is headed:

Proposal for a weekly allowance to the Poor persons belonging to the said Parish having large families in consequence of the High price of Flour and other provisions:

Adopted at a Vestry meeting held this 14 Day of

> December 1799 as follows ... That whereas their shall be a man and wife and two children or a man and two children the Guardian shall allow them four Gallons of Bread and Flour at after the rate of Ten Shillings for Bushell and the parish pay the over plush and an additional Gallon for every aditional Child under Ten years of Age. The Guardian shall grant them a written order to every such Poor person for them to deal with who they Pleas ... to commence on Sunday next the 17 Instant.
>
> It Signed by us present at the Vestry this 14 Day of November 1799.

Then follow the signatures or marks of the parish officers. In spite of the illiteracy of these minutes they show that Puttenham adopted the Speenhamland system in the hope of solving the problem of poor relief. Yet the Overseers were clutching at straws. It is when we enter the 19th century that the full horror of the situation appears in the documents relating to Puttenham. The Overseers had formed a union with Ash, supplemented wages out of the rates, given relief in kind, and yet the poor rate rose. In 1796 it was 7s. 6d. in the £, in 1801 15s., in 1810 8s. 6d., in 1812 9s.

The accounts of Richard Fludder show how desperately he and his fellow Overseers tried to stem the tide of poverty by money payments at the church:

Widow Edwards	5 weeks	12s. 6d.
Widow Swansby	5 weeks	12s. 6d.
Widdow Fludder	5 weeks	12s. 6d.

Sometimes help in kind was given and the record of this seems to cover almost everything. Bedsteads and bed-clothes, boots of all kinds, waistcoats, trowsers, straw hats, stockings, 'buttins' or, for 'Edward's boy and Browne's boy' clothing, firing and even housing. At the bottom of a bill from Pannell for 'frustians and trowsers' appears this quaint little note to the Overseer, 'Sir/I have received 40 Prs. and a half shoes of Mr. May and have sent 35 Pairs and a half'. One wonders who was to receive the half! Sometimes relief was given to those who were ill:

William Marshall—ill	5s.
Daniel Harding—fell	4s.
William Serle in Distress	4s.
Dame Harding in Distress	4s.

It is interesting to note that all these payments were made at the church, showing how the Church played a secular as well as a religious part in the village; this is emphasized by the fact that bastardy charges were also payable by the father of the child to the Overseer at the church.

It was the work of the Constable to seek out the father of a bastard child, but having discovered him it was the Overseer who had to arrange for the woman to go to the House of Industry to have the child, and it was he who had to see that the child was maintained and, if possible, place the mother in employment. It was a difficult time for young people, since poverty prevented the man from maintaining a wife, so the inevitable happened. Some women bore two or even three bastard children. Members of the family of Budd frequently came before the Justices of the Peace to declare themselves with child and to name the father—Harriet Budd gave birth to a bastard male child in 1823 and another in 1827. Charlotte Budd bore a male child in 1827 and Mary Budd a boy in the same year and lastly Sarah Budd was the mother of an unspecified child in 1839. Not only the Budds, however, bore illegitimate children; Sarah Chester in 1825 and Hannah Woods in 1829 were among others. The fathers of these children had to pay maternity charges of £2 and a weekly allowance for the child, generally 2s., until the child could maintain itself· the mother paid 6d. a week and the poor rate stood the rest. Although the problem of bastardy was a serious one it was not in the same category as that of settlement. It was here that the tragedy of the poor law administration showed most clearly.

From Settlement Orders in the possession of the Puttenham and Wanborough History Society we learn much of human misery. Paupers and their families are moved from Yorkshire to Puttenham or from Puttenham to Devonshire to get settlement. Sometimes the children are very young, sometimes there is a baby of only a few weeks, sometimes the mother is pregnant. Frequently they were sent out in midwinter. The pauper carts were supposed to be covered, but often enough the canvas would have holes in it, which would allow the bitter wind to penetrate: 12 to 15 miles a day was about the distance travelled, and the night's lodging would be a workhouse. The carrier was paid an overall sum for the journey and the more he could make out of depriving the paupers of food, except the bare minimum, the better it was for him. At the end of these nightmare journeys there was only the workhouse and no hope. In 1822 the Officers of East Stone House in Devonshire were ordered to remove from Puttenham Catherine Baker, widow, her two children—Mary aged two and a baby aged two months. The order was issued on 21 December and it is harrowing to think of this poor woman and her two tiny children being taken by the pauper cart from parish to parish in midwinter. One wonders in which workhouse en route she woke up on Christmas Day. In 1829 the Overseers of Wigan in Lancashire wrote to the Puttenham Officers demanding the removal of Hannah Woods, who was starving and ill. She was unable to get work because of 'business failures', they said. Hannah Woods must have arrived in Puttenham, for on 4 April 1829 a bastardy order was served on Peter Roe of Wigan. The child was born in the House of Industry at Ash and later Hannah Woods is found working at the *Jolly Farmer,* probably to support her child. Another removal notice in 1828 from the Overseers of Napperton in Yorkshire, to their opposite numbers in Puttenham, demanded that James Ellis, his wife and six children should be received, as Puttenham was their place of settlement. And so the wretched system continued cruelly and uneconomically and Puttenham was no more humane than any other village; notices concerning the despatch or reception of paupers appear from Compton, Camberwell, Elstead, Guildford, Southampton and Hammersmith, apart from those already mentioned.

Still the cost of poor relief was rising and by 1813 the poor rate was standing at 10s. 6d. in the £ and the House of Industry at Ash was being carefully watched for overspending during the 1820s and 1830s. The number of meetings between the Guardians of Ash, of Puttenham and the Guardian of the House of Industry increased in the hope of reducing the expenses. The cost of paupers was based on the price of flour—when this was 14s. a bushel the charge for the week per person was 3s. 7½d. and when it was 12s. a bushel, maintenance was 3s. 4½d. The bills were submitted regularly to the Puttenham Overseers and occasionally there is a plea from Lambard the Master of the Ash House of Industry asking for his salary. Sometimes there are transport bills in connection with paupers passing through to their place of settlement and cost of board and lodging for the unfortunate travellers.

The multifarious duties of the Guardians which appear in the documents and the illiteracy which is often shown give a picture of harassed men doing a thankless and overwhelming task, unpaid. No wonder they only held office for a year at a time. Yet without them the parochial administration of a national problem could never have been achieved. It was not only in Puttenham that the Overseers or Guardians of the Poor, functioned, but in every parish in England the same work was being carried out by these generally able, but often illiterate men. Instead of noting their shortcomings we must admire their public spirit in trying to cope with a desperate situation. Whether those who framed the Poor Law Amendment Act of 1834 did as valuable work for the nation as the Overseers did for the parish is questionable—in the long run, yes, but for the pauper the situation became more intolerable, as Dickens's *Oliver Twist* reveals.

NOTES

1. These documents are in the possession of the Puttenham and Wanborough History Society.
2. Document in the possession of the Puttenham and Wanborough History Society.
3. Poor Rate Account Book for Puttenham in the possession of the Puttenham and Wanborough History Society.
4. Minute in the above Poor Rate Account Book.
5. W.E. Tate, *The Parish Chest,* 3rd ed., Cambridge 1969, p.304.
6. Mavis Batey, *Life Let Us Cherish,* Farnham Papers, 2, Farnham Branch Workers Educational Association, 1965, p.7.

X

PAROCHIAL ADMINISTRATION II
THE WAYWARDENS

POOR LAW ADMINISTRATION was the most important, but not the only responsibility of the parish. The upkeep of the roads was a necessary task and extant records show the efforts made to maintain them. By the Statute of Labourers of 1555 a Surveyor of Highways had to be appointed in every parish, unpaid, and he had to order all landowners or owners of draft-horses to give four days' work on the roads per annum. Later, when appointed a new Surveyor, or Waywarden, had to take over the accounts of his predecessor, survey all the roads three times a year, organize the labour available, obtain the materials, collect the dues for the turnpike, if one existed, report to the Justices the work they had done, and specify those who did not carry out their orders for the upkeep of the roads.

W.E. Tate considers that some counties are rich in these Waywardens accounts. Surrey, he says, has a few;[1] out of those few Puttenham has quite a number, some of which are very well worth studying. Among these are several 'Johnson's Surveyor of the Highways Account-Books'. In the front of each volume there are directions to Waywardens, also called Surveyors of the Highways. These detail how roads should be prepared, what materials should be used, how they should be utilized, what implements must be available, the best way to effect drainage and what hedges and trees should be cut. Then the Waywarden is given a warning that he must enter all details of the work carried out, the expenses of all repairs and the wages paid; furthermore he must allow any ratepayer, who requires it, facilities for inspecting the accounts. The penalty for failing in his duty was £5. If Waywardens were determined to avoid this calamity they had to keep the most detailed accounts of the roads which had been repaired during the year, the men employed and their assignments, and the wages paid. At the end of his year the Waywarden had to give a report on his work. Then came the signatures of the Justices of the Peace that they had checked the accounts and, lastly, the certificate signed by the Churchwardens that these had been presented to the Vestry. The work of the Waywardens would be enough to daunt any ratepaying parishioner and the reports of these men show that they were often illiterate. One wonders how they coped with the intricacies of the assignment.

From other documents in the possession of the Puttenham and Wanborough History Society the work of the Puttenham Waywardens can be followed. By the statute of 1555 all able-bodied villagers were expected to work at least four days per annum on the roads. There is a record of this duty in Puttenham in 1769. A Waywarden's list of this date shows the use of 29 teams and 97 labourers, most of which are marked 'paid', but some are marked 'duty', probably signifying pauper labour.[2] At the beginning of the 19th century it was obviously decided that a highway rate was necessary. Accordingly, a rate of 6d. was imposed and so it remained until 1859 when it went up to 9d. This rate was levied on owners of properties assessed at over £2. The number of ratepayers and the amount expected was then recorded and, when it was approved by the Justices, it was the duty of the Warden to collect it. Once he had collected the rate, as assessed, he had to get workmen and materials to the places in Puttenham's six miles of road which needed repairing, to see that the work was done, and to pay the teams and labourers. Detailed accounts are to be found in Johnson's Surveyors Account-Book, but before these were available accounts were kept on scraps of paper and from them and the books we can piece together the very difficult year which a Waywarden had to face. The Account Books of the Waywardens for Puttenham date from 1842 to 1860, although some years are missing, but using these and the scraps of paper on which are written bills and accounts from 1769 it is possible to envisage the work which was done in the village at intervals from that date.

There appear to have been three kinds of labour employed on the roads in Puttenham. Day Labour was extensively used, which included the work of the ratepayers, who had no teams to supply and who preferred to work rather than find substitutes whom they would have had to pay; women, who were generally employed in stone sorting; and paupers, who were placed on road work by the

Puttenham Common

parish and received 1s. a day. The work of these day labourers was generally unsatisfactory, since they were unwilling employees and used their time unproductively. A writer in 1696 calls these workers on the King's Highway 'The King's Loiterers'.[3] The entries in the Account Books indicate how the Waywardens paid their day labour:

Charles Cobbett	2 days on the road 4s.	1812
George Smith	2 days on the road 5s.	1812
'Payment to men on the road 5s.'		1822

Several payments to women appear: James Smith paid

4 women 1 day each picking stones 2s. 8d.	1822

This amounts to 8d. a day each for the women—surely sweated labour and no suggestion of equal pay for equal work. Again, Richard Fludder paid 'Dame Flutter 3 days picking stones 2.0'. It is not difficult to imagine the back-breaking work these women undertook for a pittance. Paupers were employed on the road for long periods since the more they earned the less they were a charge on the parish. They were usually paid 1s. or 1s. 2d. a day and in the Surveyors Account-Book, kept by Richard Fludder in 1861, there is a long list of men who can be identified as paupers from the list of the Guardians of the Poor. William Chalcroft works 11½ days in one month and receives 19s. 2d. John Clark works 24 days in June and receives 25s. 8d.

Then there was team work, usually organized by the farmers. They would be expected to send horses, carts and labourers and the payment was generally at the rate of 4s. per horse. These horses and carts were used to bring the materials from the quarries to the roads on which they were to be used. It was now that the Surveyor had to remember his instructions as to how the stones were to be laid, the drainage provided, and the surface secured. The entries for this work are numerous; for example, in 1822 George Ellis was paid by 'D. Simmonds, Surveyor' for 'team work at Lascomb, Hook Lane, Street' and for 'carting stones and chalk' from November 1822 to June 1823 '£20 6s. 0d.'. Bills for carting by these teams enable us to discover the quarries from which the materials were obtained—stone from East Field and Further East Field, flint from the Hog's Back, iron-stone from Elstead and Southfield, Barget stone from the Stone Pit and chalk from the Chalk Pit, south of the Hog's Back. Stone from East Field and Further East Field appears in a bill for 64 loads in 1822 and 1824;

41 loads of flints from the Hog's Back occur in 1822; chalk from Chalk Pit is listed in 1823 and stone from 'Suttle Lane' in 1828.

Thirdly, the Account Books have entries dealing with contract work. This was probably carried out by some of the land-owners and large farmers as a financial proposition. A bill was presented to the Waywardens by Litzenburg for supply of teams for road work from 1828 to 1830, and another for 'team on the road at 16s. a day from November 1821 to May 1822.'

Payment for road work was not the only disbursement which a Waywarden had to make, for he had also to employ specialists. Ditching was a skilled job as it was necessary to get the right depth and the right fall for the water; tree lopping and hedge cutting needed a trained man; carpenters were required for repairing gates (known as hatches); blacksmiths were employed to repair latches, implements, and to sharpen becks and 'mad hooks' (mattocks). There are many bills from Fludder, the blacksmith, for the repair of iron work and from Penfold, the carpenter, for supplying wooden handles for the implements. Bricklayers were needed. One brought bricks from Wanborough, for which he was paid £1 per 100, and he used these for mending the gutter in Puttenham Street. One further set of bills is interesting, namely, for the supply of beer to those working on the road. Apparently the Waywardens paid for this and there are several bills from J. Litzenburg of the *Jolly Farmer* for 'a pot of beer 6d.' supplied to all those working on the roads. These bills generally extend over six months. W.E. Tate states that in some places those doing statute labour on the roads were supplied with a certain amount of beer and he cites the case of Pavenham, Bedfordshire, where beer was supplied to the men according to a scale drawn up in 1774.[4] The Puttenham Waywardens were equally thoughtful; Litzenburg was instructed to supply the drinks—and how welcome they must have been!

According to the reckoning of Richard Fludder, Puttenham had six miles of local roads. There was one other obligation, however, for the Waywarden in addition to the upkeep of the roads and that was the composition-rate payable to the Farnham and Guildford Turnpike Trust. These Turnpike Trusts were established to improve the main trunk roads. At first the labour for the project was recruited from the villages through which the turnpikes ran, but it became too much of an imposition on the villagers, so a composition rate was agreed upon for all turnpikes and Puttenham was pleased to be able to enter into such an agreement. Consequently there are receipts from the Farnham Turnpike for £1 8s. 6d., the yearly composition rate paid instead of sending statute labour. There is one receipt for £2 7s. 0d. Whether this was because of some deterioration in the condition of the turnpike is not clear, but it seems to have been paid without a murmur.

When the Waywarden came to the end of his year of office he had to make a report on all the work he had done and the payments he had made. These reports show how little educated the Wardens were and one wonders how they had managed to find their way through the intricacies of the year. In answer to the question as to which parts of the roads he had repaired and how he had done it one Warden wrote tersely 'All have been done what was necessary' and another said 'all as been Done as was Necessary'.[5]

How successful the Waywardens were in keeping the roads of Puttenham there is no means of telling, but one wonders if they were any better maintained than were those described by William Cobbett in 1822, when he rode through Surrey. 'Frightful conditions of roads', he wrote, 'lanes pretty between steep banks', but 'wheel tracks about 6 inches deep', 'indescribable dirt and mire of the roads'.[6]

THE VILLAGE CONSTABLE

As W.E. Tate so truly says, the Constable 'was an odd job man'.[7] He appears in all branches of parish administration. He deals with vagrants; with the County Rate; apprehension of fathers of bastard children before or after birth; he attends petty sessions with parochial lists; apprehends criminals; summons the militia and keeps the town arms, probably in the church tower. The Constable had as many and as varied duties as the Churchwarden and, like him, his office was a relic of medieval times—that of the Tithing-man, whose work was never clearly defined.

In Puttenham, according to the records possessed by the Puttenham and Wanborough History Society, the Constable was undoubtedly a jack-of-all-trades and often almost illiterate. The following are typical entries. 'From G. Penfold, Constabel. Relief of man and wife ill', 1821. 'James Smith Relieved a Womman' and again, in beautiful copperplate writing, 'Releiving man and two children'. In 1834 Thomas Smyth, Constable to the Parish asked the parish for £10 13s. 3d., the County Rate, 'as I am under the necessity of paying it in A few days'. In 1829 we read, 'To the Constable of Puttenham from G.W. Onslow' (a Justice of the Peace) that Hannah Woods has 'declared herself to be with child ... and that Peter Roe of Wigan ... is the father ... I (Onslow) do, therefore, command you immediately to apprehend the said Peter Roe and to bring him before me or some other of His Majesty's J.P.s ... to find security to indemnify the said Parish' (Puttenham). Whether the Constable had to go to Wigan to carry out the order is not stated, but in all probability he had to make the long journey. In 1821 George Penfold, another Constable, made entries in his bill presented to the parish that are indicative of his work and his illiteracy: 'Taking the Overs' Seers List and Delivering the Warrants from the bench 5s.', and again, 'Attenting the bench with Waywardings Lists 5s.' and, using alternative spelling, 'Atenting the bench with Waywardings Lists 5s'. Yet another entry is: 'Dec$^{d.}$ 14 [14 December] Executing the Warrant in the Knight [sic] for seeking vagrants with 2 men 2s. 6d.' In 1822 Penfold was still Constable and claimed 'Sept$^{br.}$ 24 Atenting the Pettey Shesons and Oath 6s.'. These last two references illustrate an important part of a Constable's work—the apprehension of anyone who had committed a felony and the presentation of anyone, so arrested, before the magistrates. As we saw, when studying the 16th century, several instances occurred of Puttenham men being called to the muster, particularly at the time of the Spanish menace under Elizabeth. It was still the work of the Constable to assemble the muster. On 23 November 1822 Penfold entered in his accounts 'Atending the Bench with the Millitia duty and Oath 6s'. The Constable could order those named to serve with the militia unless they could obtain substitutes. A certificate of 17 February 1818, issued by the Clerk to the Southwark Court of Lieutenancy to the Royal Surrey Militia (First Regiment), states that James Palmer has provided Edward Strudwick as his substitute, James Palmer 'having been balloted to serve in the Militia'.[8]

An account from James Smith, Constable, to the parish of Puttenham 1828, is interesting; it includes an item for 'Atending farnham bench' and another for 'Constable Staff—2s.' The first of these shows that the Constable had to be prepared to attend at the

Magistrate's Court, either in Guildford or in Farnham; unless he had a horse he would have had to walk roughly eight miles there and back in either case. It was no sinecure to be a parish administrator in any capacity, but, perhaps, the most hated office of all was that of the Constable. The second reference above, to the Constable's staff is probably for some small repair, but the fact that it is mentioned shows that the Constable's staff, a sign that he was a preserver of the peace, was used by the Puttenham holder of the office and was, quite probably, attached to the door of his house to indicate that he was a man of authority. The work of the Constable, as that of other office-holders in the parish of Puttenham—which is illustrated by extant documents—appears to have been very closely in line with the practice in other villages throughout the country.

MEDICAL SERVICE

The medical practitioner was not an officer of the parish administration, but he was very necessary to it. The first example of which there is any evidence is Edward Jackson, probably from Godalming. He submitted his yearly bill for May 1822 to 'The Parish', but it was the Overseer of the Poor of Puttenham who was responsible for its payment. In it Mr. Jackson asked for his yearly basic salary of £10 and then listed other visits which he had made—'Applications and attendance for several weeks to an extensive burn to the arms, legs, thighs & Breast—Budds £2 2s. 0d.', 'A journey and attendance in Labour—Mrs. Pink—£1 6s. 0d.' In 1828 Jackson presented a bill for the months of March, April, May—'Journey 5s., Mixture & pills 5s.'. However, in June of the same year there appears to have been a change of physicians, or, perhaps, the practice was divided. Messrs. Balchin and Haines now come on the scene.

Balchin and Haines submitted a bill to Puttenham Parish in June 1828 for 'reducing a severe fracture, mixture Mr. Chalcroft, aperient and doses and journey to Ash 10s. 6d.' Evidence appears elsewhere that Chalcroft was a pauper, hence the physician's journey to Ash, where his patient would be an inmate of the House of Industry. In a receipt for their yearly bill for 1829 we discover that Messrs. Balchin and Haines were physicians in Godalming. It is addressed from Godalming and acknowledges the payment from 'Mr. May, Guardian of the Parish of Puttenham of

£15 7s. 0d. for one years attendance and Extras'. In 1829 the yearly bill of Balchin and Haines is very full: 'Bleeding Master Chalcroft 1. 0, A Mixture 2. 6, A Journey to Ash Mrs. Searle 7. 6, Three aperient doses 3. 0, A box of Pills 2. 6, A saline mixture 2. 6'. The list continues in the same way for the year, and from it we learn that medicines were expensive, for 2s. 6d. was a large sum to pay for pills and mixtures and a journey to Ash which cost 7s. 6d. must have made calling the physician an expensive affair. The journey had to be done on horseback and from Godalming to Ash would have taken a considerable time. The basic salary of £10 paid for medical attendance by the Overseers of Puttenham seems to have been a representative figure since W.E. Tate refers to a vestry medical contract from Cardington, Beds., amounting to £10 10s. 0d.[9]

Nurses, such as we know them today, did not exist. They were generally the hags of the village who nursed when they had to do so, and happily laid out the dead, since for this office they received good payment. According to tradition they did little for the living whom they were supposed to nurse, but they were always in evidence at funerals. They would walk behind the coffin to the church, attend at the graveside and hold the hats of the mourners. Immediately after the funeral they would return to the house of the deceased and wait to be paid.[10] 'The Puttenham Sharks'—as the village nurses were called—were not remembered for their skill in nursing which appears to have had little value.

The administrative work carried out in the villages by uneducated men (with the exception of the physician), who were bound to serve, illustrates the effort which each parish made to deal with its problems and one must admire the complicated work which they undertook. Judging by the Puttenham documents the same men were called upon at intervals to serve in one capacity or another, but whether they were victims of their own efficiency or whether they were a village oligarchy to which father, son and grandson belonged, it is not possible to tell. Whichever was the case, there is no reason to think that the parochial administration of Puttenham was any less successful than that of other villages in South-east England.

NOTES

1. W.E. Tate, *The Parish Chest,* 3rd ed., p.249.
2. Kerry, vol.viii, p.155.
3. W.E. Tate, *The Parish Chest,* p.245: 'The Cottagers ... used the occasion (of unpaid labour on the roads) for gathering alms from the passers by'.
4. W.E. Tate, *The Parish Chest,* p.174.
5. From Waywarden's Account Books in possession of Puttenham and Wanborough History Society.
6. W. Cobbett, *Rural Rides,* Everyman ed., p.135.
7. W.E. Tate, *The Parish Chest,* p.187.
8. Certificate in possession of the Puttenham and Wanborough History Society.
9. W.E. Tate, *The Parish Chest,* p.167.
10. Kerry, vol.vi, pp.77-78.

XI

AGRICULTURE IN PUTTENHAM IN THE NINETEENTH CENTURY

IN COMPANY with the other small villages south of the Hog's Back, Puttenham continued as a quiet agricultural community during the first half of the 19th century. It had little connection with the outside world and was in no way involved in any machine-breaking disturbances. However, for one brief moment, in 1805, it entered the national arena. This was at the time when war had broken out once more between England and France. On 14 March there was issued from the 'General Sessions of the Peace of our Sovereign Lord the King' an assessment of fines payable by each village in lieu of men who should have been sent to the armed forces. The 'Military Assessment for the County of Surrey' ordered a payment for each man who failed to register. Puttenham was assessed at £37.[1] Presumably the village paid the amount and, having done so, sank once more into its accustomed obscurity.

The census returns for 1821 and 1831 gave a fairly clear picture of Puttenham as an agricultural village in the first three decades of the century. The one of 1821 carried out by Edward Holloway, the parish clerk, shows a population of 389 persons in 83 families, 64 of these families being engaged in agriculture. Ten years later Richard Fludder, Overseer, gives a population of 392, only three more than in 1821. Out of 77 families mentioned in this census 52 were employed in agriculture. It is interesting to note that in both returns it is stated that all the houses are occupied.[2] It is with this agricultural and unobtrusive background that we must see Puttenham in the 19th century.

The farmers had a difficult time in the first three decades of this century, William Cobbett wrote violently of the decline in agriculture and Lord Ernle draws gloomy pictures of rural distress: 'Between 1815 and the accession of Queen Victoria falls one of the blackest periods of English farming'.[3] Judging by the increase in the poor rate the agricultural labourer, everywhere, was badly hit. Recent research, however, has shown that the picture was not as black as historians once painted it. Dr. E.L. Jones considers that Ernle coloured his judgments by not differentiating between the heavy clay soils, which were often unproductive, and the lighter soils which were able to weather the storm.[4] Puttenham, lying as it does on easy cultivable soil, probably did not suffer as much as some other parts of the country. In spite of the increasing pauper rate there is only one agricultural failure mentioned. In 1834 George Smith was declared bankrupt and his lands were returned to the Lord of the Manor. Nor did the village suffer from large-scale enclosures. Certainly there were none carried out by Act of Parliament, and there is evidence of only one 'appropriation of common land by consent of the vestry'. The records of the Court Baron held in Puttenham, however, show a few minor enclosures. On 17 October 1817, 'William Keen admitted to lands of his father, William Keen, including a certain amount of the waste land now enclosed called Wortham Common'. On 19 July 1819, William Keen 'conveyed to James Fox ... land from the waste near Perryman's Mead now enclosed'.[5]

The 'Appropriation of Land' by consent of the Vestry in 1794 is interesting. W.E. Tate shows there is little evidence of Vestry Enclosure extant today,[6] so it is worth considering the only one recorded in Puttenham. In this year Nathaniel Snell, although living at Hampton, Seale, had bought the lordships of the Puttenham Manors from Thomas Parker. He was anxious to enclose some common land and a pond at Gatwick. Common land was important to the villager as he had a right to graze his cattle there and also it supplied him with litter for his stock and peat for his fire. Consequently, it was a matter of great concern if a proposal was made for any such enclosure. However, Nathaniel Snell was determined to carry out his scheme, but with strict legality. The procedure to be followed was that a notice of appropriation of land had to be affixed to the church door on three Sundays before the matter came before the Vestry, which then had to meet and give its consent. In May 1794 a notice was pinned on the door of the church at Puttenham calling a Vestry meeting to consider the proposed enclosure of land at Gatwick desired by Nathaniel Snell. This took place on 30 May. Snell gained the consent of the Vestry, and the enclosure was recorded in the Minutes of the Court Baron for 7 June 1794, where it was stated that this land was not to be subject to heriot. The document permitting the enclosure was drawn up in the following terms:

> At a Vestry meeting of the Parishioners of the Parish of Puttenham in the County of Surrey, held in the Parish Church pursuant to public notice in the said Church for three Sundays last past, on Friday, the thirtieth day of May 1794. The parishioners present at this meeting having taken into consideration a proposition made to them by Nathaniel Snell, Esq. ... for taking and enclosing a certain part of the commons ... by estimation twenty acres ... lying near unto the Pond of the said Mr. Snell ... he paying the purchase money ... amounting to one hundred and twenty five pounds ... do here by ... and consent to agree to the enclosure.[7]

The land to be enclosed was probably to be used for grazing, and the ponds for watering the animals. The enclosure would prevent the animals from being contaminated by others grazing on the common land or drinking at the pond. In return for this concession, apart from the £125, Snell gave part of a meadow to Keen, a yeoman of Rodsall, and allowed him the use of the mill stream for watering his animals in Gatwick Meadows. Furthermore, the parishioners were to be permitted to enclose common land between Whitfield House and Froghole Lane and land adjoining the turnpike, should they wish to do so. The purchase money of £125 was to be given to the Churchwardens and Overseers to use as they saw fit. Such money was usually put towards poor relief. There is no evidence of how the money was allocated but, considering the Overseers are mentioned, it seems likely that it was used for poor relief in some way. W.E. Tate refers to the authorisation of enclosure by the Vestry at Ham, Surrey, and at Keston, Kent. In the latter case a perpetual annuity of £10 to the poor of the parish is mentioned.[8]

There is no record of any machine-breaking or riots on account of the introduction of threshing machines, so it is probable that the old type of farming continued. Seed was still broadcast, harvesting was done with sickle or scythe, and threshing was carried out in the barns with flails. Kerry relates the story of Parson Williams, curate of Puttenham from 1811 to 1823, who 'in

The hop kilns, The Street

lieu of a seed lip once sowed the Parsonage Field with wheat out of an old fish kettle suspended round his neck with a cord. Winter [the parish clerk] declares he could hardly harrow after him for laughing, but although the whole process was gone through before it was light, there never was a better crop of wheat in that field—not a yard was missed'.[9] The records of the Courts Baron show how the medieval system of husbandry was still practised. On 5 October 1789 William Sparks was presented to the Court 'for having cut two loads of Fearn on Puttenham Great Common and for having carried it away to the farm at Puttenham on the Fourth of August'. He was fined 5s. a load, the bracken 'having been cut before the twenty-fifth day of August'. At the same Court Edward Keen was presented 'for having erected several sheep pens on part of the Common or Waste of the Lord of the Manor'. So, too, was 'James Reynolds for having turned out Hogs upon the Common and Waste lands of the Manor'.[10]

The farming community of Puttenham seems to have weathered the storm of the first third of the 19th century and there is no record of any hard times, except when weather conditions caused harvest failures. By the middle of the century hop growing had become a paying crop. There were several hop kilns built in the village, showing that a considerable acreage must have been given over to hops. The only kilns used until recently date from about 1800. There was no restriction on hop production then, as there is now, and it was not necessary to employ extra skilled labour for the harvest. A diary kept by Marshall, Allden's shepherd, states that he was sent hop-picking when not engaged with his sheep.[11]

A change in the general agricultural policy of the village appears after 1860, which helped farmers over the time of the 'Great Depression', 1870-1900. This was the adoption of mixed farming instead of dependence on wheat, the price of which reached rock bottom owing to the influx of American grain. Sheep farming, also, became more important and, quoting Marshall's diary again, there is a reference to his purchase for Mr. Hewett, of Priory Farm, of 'Hampshires, Southdowns, Dorsets, Downs' and unnamed sheep from Chichester, Reading, Salisbury and Marlborough. 'In April [? 1885] between the 9th and 18th', he drove '279 sheep of different breeds to Guildford market'. Cattle were by this time also an agricultural undertaking, and a catalogue of a sale of the live and dead stock at the Home Farm, Puttenham, shows 14 two-year-old shorthorn steers and five cows and heifers for auction. Sam Marshall, of Priory Farm, bought milking cows, as the corn crops were bad, he said, and retailed milk at 2d. a pint.[12] This move towards mixed farming was more generally undertaken on the light soils of South-east England, but, in a lesser degree, it extended to Cornwall in the South and Cumberland in the North.[13] Thus the farmers in Puttenham followed the newer trends, even if only in a small way. Furthermore, the new network of railways made it easier to despatch livestock to London or to other markets. Marshall, the shepherd, speaks of bringing sheep to Wanborough by train and then driving them to Puttenham. Also, at the end of the century, hops were sent to the Borough instead of to Wey Hill. As a result of rail transport farmers could avail themselves of the better prices offered in London.

Another venture in agriculture which appeared in the latter years of the century was horticulture. This was undertaken in many parts of England at this time to offset the slump in wheat, but Puttenham had an added incentive—the needs of the army at Aldershot. Sam Marshall, in 1895, again saw his advantage and, with Strudwick to help him, began to grow vegetables and potatoes in his fields below the Hog's Back. He was soon engaged in a lucrative trade with Aldershot. He acquired an engine and two trucks and made his deliveries to the camp. He then filled the trucks with manure from the stables at Aldershot and returned to Puttenham to improve the fertility of his land and to grow better vegetables.

Marshall, who began work on a farm in 1874, gives us a picture of farming in the last third of the 19th century. He was first employed to scare rooks from the fields, which had been freshly sown, for which he was paid 8d. a day. He proudly describes the four-horse teams with which he learned to plough and tells of the carter's pride in his horses, which were decorated with horse bells when they took the corn to the mills. Later Marshall was employed as a foreman of potato diggers. He had, he says, 'as many as seventy forks digging'. Corn harvest, he wrote in 1942, was a slow business in 1886; there were no machines and everything was done by hand. Casual labour would be brought in and everyone, including the women, would have to work hard to get the corn cut, stooked and stacked before the weather should break. Wages were low even in the monetary value of that day. In the 'nineties an agricultural labourer was paid 15s. a week, but cottage rents were low—usually 1s. 6d. or 2s. a week.[14] By the end of the century this medieval policy was gradually being superseded by more modern methods. An inventory of the machinery at the Home Farm in 1908 shows the passing of one era and the beginning of another. The items for sale included 3 waggons, 3 scotch carts and 7 cart-horses, but, also, a McCormick Self-binder, a mowing machine and a 14-coulter Corn and Seed Drill. Some fields, it is stated, were spread entirely with manure, but two were dressed with artificial fertilizers; hand-hoeing is specifically mentioned as having been carried out and the crops, which are interesting, were mangolds, barley or swedes after oats and mustard after tares. In those days oats were essential for horse feeding, but with the disappearance of the Shire breeds of farm horses the cultivation of oats has almost ended in the South-east.

By the first decade of the 20th century farming was just entering the modern era of mechanization, although it was not until after World War I that the tractor, the cutter-and-binder and the swath-turner became common. It was even later than this that artificial fertilizers came into general use. In spite of the fact that traditional methods of farming lingered on, the farmers in England, and with them those of Puttenham, weathered the troubles of the Great Depression and were able to feed the population of the country during the war of 1914-1918.

NOTES

1. Surrey Archaeological Collections, lii, p.61.
2. Kerry, vol.ii, p.162.
3. Lord Ernle, *Farming Past and Present,* 6th edn., p.322.
4. E.L. Jones, *Development of English Agriculture 1815-1873,* (Studies in English Economic History, London 1968) p.14.
5. Minutes of the Court Baron of Puttenham Priory and Puttenham Bury in possession of the present Lord of the Manors.
6. W.E. Tate, *The Parish Chest,* 3rd ed., Cambridge 1969, p.267.
7. Kerry, vol.ii, p.181. Kerry says that this document was 'copied from a loose sheet of paper preserved in a rate book (dated 1782-1793) kept with the Churchwardens' accounts, but lent me by Mr. Hewett who had a loan of it from Mr. Shrubb, Churchwarden'. The whereabouts of the original is not now known.
8. W.E. Tate, *The Parish Chest* p.267.
9. Kerry, vol.iii, p.153.
10. Minutes of the Court Baron of Puttenham Priory and Puttenham Bury.
11. Diary in the possession of his great niece, Miss Marshall.
12. Samuel Marshall, *The Life of a Successful Farmer in Surrey,* Farnham 1942, p.12.
13. E.L. Jones, *Development of English Agriculture 1815-1873,* p.22.
14. Samuel Marshall, *The Life of a Successful Farmer in Surrey,* p.7.

XII

CHURCH AND VILLAGE IN THE NINETEENTH CENTURY

AT THE WEST END of the Church of St. John the Baptist, Puttenham, are some water colours by the early 19th century artist, Hassell, which show how the restoration of the church after the fire reflected the current theological ideas of the period. The great two-decker pulpit dominates the whole of the interior, while the altar is insignificant and in the nave the great box pews are shown where, probably, those who wished could sleep unnoticed whilst the parson expounded the Word in his long sermon.

By the late 1830s, however, under the influence of the Oxford Movement new ecclesiological ideas were current and, in 1841, these were sponsored by the Camden Society in Cambridge. The Society is probably responsible for much preservation work amongst decaying churches, but the enthusiasm with which its ideas were accepted caused a great deal of ecclesiastical vandalism throughout the country. The central position of the altar was the most important part of the Society's architectural teaching. It is possible to see the work of the Camden Society's devotees in the majority of the medieval churches of today, no less than in Puttenham. In 1861, the Revd. W.G. Duckworth, the rector, and his Churchwardens enthusiastically supported these new ideas and, having arranged to have Mattins in the school room at Puttenham and Evensong in the afternoon at Wanborough, they set about 'restoring' the 800-year-old church of St. John the Baptist. They pulled down the east end and rebuilt it with steps to the chancel and two more to the sanctuary and then placed the altar at the top of these. They lowered the floor in the Priory chapel, they ripped out most of the windows, placed a new pulpit where the double-decker had been, put a new font at the west end and rebuilt the south porch. In July 1862, after a year's 'restoration', the church was re-opened, 'the bishop of Winchester preached and a public luncheon and tea were held under a tent on the Heath'.[1] There seems to have been great satisfaction with the work and the village appears to have appreciated it, since 'The Clerical Rover' writing in the *West Surrey Times,* 6 March 1869, speaks with enthusiasm of the service he attended at Puttenham and remarks that the the 'Church was quite full'. He also mentions that the blacksmith's daughter was at the organ and describes the gentry in their frock coats, whilst the farm labourers, sitting at the back of the church in the new pitch pine seats, wore clean white smocks. It was a type of service that could have been seen almost anywhere in England in the late 19th century. A change, however, was near, for a more sacramental approach to worship was appearing. Sacrament Sunday, when communion had been celebrated once a quarter, was gradually being superseded by Sacrament Sunday once a month; and in 1885 Puttenham went even further, when the Revd. George Clarke became rector and introduced weekly communion. The weekly communion is still the practice, but the architectural changes organized by his predecessor do not please, even after a hundred years, either in Puttenham or any other of the many churches 'restored' under the influence of the ecclesiology of the Camden Society.

The church, however, was not only concerned with changes in churchmanship and architecture; it was well aware of its responsibility for education. During the late 1820s and 1830s the incumbents of parishes throughout the country eagerly sought the help of the National Society and other bodies for school buildings since they realized the depth of the ignorance of the poor under their care. As the century progressed it became obvious that the inadequate classroom accommodation necessitated more funds and better teachers. In 1870 compulsory education added to their difficulties and Vestry meetings were frequent and sometimes despairing. Then came the system of payment by results, when government grants were given only on the recommendation of school inspectors. It is understandable that, in order to get the grant, backward children were 'unavoidably absent'. The incumbent was always harassed by his school problems, which were increased by financial worries, difficult managers, poorly trained teachers, inadequate syllabuses and, sometimes, the fear that the school might lose church supervision as a result of lack of funds. These pressures were widespread and Puttenham was no exception.

The earliest reference we have to a school in the village is of one kept by the rector, Thomas Swift, in 1738.[2] There is no evidence to show how many attended or who they were. In 1796 George Eastmond was buried and Kerry adds to the entry 'Schoolmaster in this parish for about 12 years'.[3] In 1829 the Revd. T.W. Richards, the rector, came face to face with the problem and appealed to the National Society for help, stating that 'there are 56 children in the parish and a schoolroom only measuring 28′ x 16′ x 10′ ' and 'so no adequate educational institute of any kind'. Furthermore, he continues, 'there is only one resident gentleman and the rector'. The National Society gave a grant of £50 and Richards raised £65 by 'Subscriptions, Preaching and begging from house to house'.[4] A one-room school was built and used for boys and girls, infants and older children, until 1872. By then the 1870 Act had been passed and action was necessary. Trustees were appointed and a piece of land obtained 'as a site for a new school for poor persons within the parish of Puttenham'. The Vestry Minute Books 1882-1919 reflect the problems of education in the village. Registers were to be checked once a month for the inspection of H.M.Is. The rector volunteered to do this in 1885. In 1888 the Monitor System, whereby the older children taught the younger ones, was instituted, but this was later condemned. Payment by results revealed poor standards and, consequently, schoolmasters and schoolmistresses were continually being dismissed.[5]

By 1902 more trouble faced the school managers and, especially, the rector, the Revd. George Clarke. The Government inspectors reported that 'the School Buildings are in a delapidated condition and unsuited for school purposes ... and the question of erecting fresh premises should engage the serious attention of the managers'.[6] The rector, following the example of his predecessor, the Revd. T.W. Richards, now had to set about raising funds. His task was not easy, as the lord of the manor had quarrelled with the National Society, and it looked as though the school would either lose its grant or its manorial support. If the former, the school would be forced to become a provided and not a church school. The rector wrote to the Society explaining his difficulties and remarking that Puttenham was a very poor parish '... agriculture was in a depressed state and the last farmer of the old type was leaving the village'. He begged the Society for the continuation of the grant. It agreed, and the grant was extended. This was added to by loans and gifts and the new school was opened in December 1903. The rector's comment on his success was 'by a venture of faith a provided school is kept out of Puttenham.'[7]

From the School Log Books 1893-1921 it is possible to visualize school life in Puttenham during this period and to realize how typical it was of other villages. They show how much time the rector devoted to the children, teaching religious knowledge and visiting the classes frequently. They note the help given by his wife in the infant department and her supervision of the needlework taught in the school. Infectious diseases are continually referred to, the prevalence of which today would be quite unthinkable; in 1896, 1897 and 1898 diphtheria is mentioned, quite casually, as having caused the death of several children in each of these years. In 1897 five children 'died of exhaustion after measles'. Whooping cough and scarlet fever also broke out in this same year. Perhaps one cause of so much illness can be related to an entry 'school closed for one day, because the cess pool overflowed into the schoolyard and cloak-passages'. In 1910 there are several notes as to gipsy children being admitted, but being sent away because they were 'unclean in body and hair'. The numerous references to bad weather in the Log Book and their connection with bad attendance reminds us that children were not brought to school by bus, but had to walk, sometimes for miles and often across muddy fields and along badly kept roads. There was no village hall, other than the school house until 1903, and consequently the school was used for village activities—the Clothing Club, the Shoe Club, and the National Deposit Friendly Society received their weekly payments here and the 'Adult Band Practised' in the classroom in the evenings.

The 1914 war brought staffing difficulties, but also some progress. Scholarships to the Grammar School at Guildford were begun in 1919 and in the same year school meals were organized by Mrs. Mowbray Howard of Hampton, Seale, as a private venture. As early as 1905 school expeditions were introduced and visits were paid to Cowes and the Crystal Palace. Two items of interest appear in the Log Book for 1915. One written by the Headmaster, Mr. King: 'I have today joined the 24th Royal Fusiliers. (Public Schools Battalion)'. The other for 22 February: 'The schools are required for billeting purposes this week consequently the children are dismissed'. When the troops left after a month's residence Mr. Porter ordered 'that the schools must be thoroughly cleaned before re-opening'.[8] Mr. King returned from the army to take up his duties once more as Headmaster. By the end of the war the struggle to bring education to 'the poor of Puttenham' had been won and the school was ready to enter the more enlightened years of the 20th century.

The 'Town' of Puttenham is described in a Terrier drawn up in 1765, which states that it 'ran from the Priory to the top of the Street and covered an area of 19 acres, 0.R., 5 Poles'.[9] This, of course, was not the full extent of the village, since fields surrounded the 'Town', but here is the setting for the lords of the manor, the squires and the people of the township, in all a population of 389 in 1821. The lords of the manor and the squires appear clearly in the various documents of the period, but the individual villagers are more difficult to distinguish. It is to see them all in their social activities, their joys and their sorrows, that we turn now to the Kerry documents.

When Thomas Parker sold the Priory estates in 1775 'together with the pews in the chancel (lately beautified)'[10] he ended over a hundred years of possession of the manors of Puttenham by members of the Inner Temple, all of whom had steered a precarious financial course by means of mortgages. The purchaser of the manor was Samuel Cornish, Admiral of the Blue and participant in naval occasions at the time of Hood and Rodney. Cornish was born Samuel Pitchford, but took the name of Cornish when his uncle, Admiral Sir Samuel Cornish, died and left him his fortune. As a result of receiving his legacy and his prize money Cornish desired a country estate; he was attracted to the Priory, probably because his wife, Mary Sumner, had lived at Shackleford and had seen how Parker had altered the Priory farmhouse into a Palladian mansion. Cornish had the money and he did not need mortgages, so he bought the estate. However, he did not buy the lordships of the manors. These were retained by Parker, when he went to Hampton Lodge, Seale, and were afterwards sold to Nathaniel Snell when he bought Hampton on Parker's death in 1791. Samuel Cornish was twice recalled to sea from Puttenham—in 1782 when he commanded H.M.S. *Arrogant* against a French and Spanish fleet in the battle of Dominica, and in 1790 when he captained the *Marlborough* in a short war against Spain. After his return from this expedition he was made Admiral of the White, or Vice Admiral, and later he reached the rank of the Red or, as we would call it today, full Admiral. This rank is noted on his tablet in the church. Unfortunately, there is no evidence of the part he played in Puttenham, although the villagers must have felt some reflected glory when they saw him take his place in his pew 'lately decorated'. Edward Long, his neighbour at Hampton, speaks of him in 1801 as 'my old friend Admiral Cornish', but remarks, after a visit to the Admiral at the Priory, that he does not 'admire the house, but thinks that the grounds are set out in a nice park-like manner'.[11] Samuel Cornish died in 1816 and was buried in the vault beneath the chancel in Puttenham Church. His very pleasant late classical monument states that 'he was a man of mild and gentle manners kind in heart and of great benevolence'. So passed the last of the picturesque owners of the Priory estate. He was succeeded by someone of quite other characteristics, whose family did not even think it necessary to raise a memorial to him. Richard Sumner portrays for us the typical straight-laced Victorian squire.

Richard Sumner was a nephew of Admiral Cornish and he bought the Priory from his aunt, Mary Cornish. He was a good landlord, maintaining his property well and was interested in the welfare of the village. His diary shows that he bought a considerable amount of property in the village, as it came on to the market, that he gave money towards building the new rectory and the school house and subscribed to the organ fund. In spite of Sumner's generous contributions to village projects, Kerry shows him to have been a dictatorial and somewhat unpleasant man. His desire to be in and not of the village appears in his determination to live in comparative isolation. He organized the demolition of the old rectory, which overlooked his house and he obtained permission from the Justices to re-route the road which ran beneath his windows, turning it to the north side of the church—its present position.[12]

Kerry gives us some anecdotes which provide an insight into the character of Richard Sumner. Kerry was working on the erection of new altar rails in 1869 when Richard Sumner entered the church through his private door in the manorial chapel, looking somewhat pleased 'if pleasure can be expressed by grunts of approval', says Kerry. However, this was quickly succeeded by displeasure at the suggestion of stained glass windows to be given to the church by the Pope family, who were only connected with Puttenham by marriage into the families of two incumbents, the Revd. Watkyn Richards and the Revd. Charles Duckworth. Those windows 'will darken the church exceedingly', muttered Richard Sumner. 'People will not be able to see their service books', he continued, 'and as for the south transept, where I sit, it is impossible even now to read in the afternoons of winter days'. Kerry appears to have been a little tactless when he said to Sumner that he thought it was kind of the Popes to give these windows. Sumner replied, 'Archdeacon Pope had no right to be buried in Puttenham churchyard, a very large piece of the churchyard has been devoted to his vault, in fact, it is large enough to hold four carcasses'. 'With that' says Kerry, 'he left the church'.[13]

As we have seen, when Parker sold the Priory to Cornish he did not sell the manorial rights, since these were taken to Seale by Parker and now belonged to the lord of the manor of Seale. Consequently, when Richard Sumner bought lands in the village he had to be admitted to a copyhold of the manor of Puttenham. On 20 August 1834, he appeared before the Court Baron of Henry Long of Hampton and was admitted 'tenant of a messuage in the Street'. Thus he did not own this property by right of freehold. His position, however, was that of a squire and the picture of his funeral given by Kerry shows that he was recognized as such and depicts a typical 19th century ceremony. Kerry writes, 'On 15 May 1873 the Sumner's family vault was opened to receive the body of Richard Sumner Esq. of Puttenham Priory'. The gentry who followed his coffin included Morton Sumner, Lord Viscount Midleton, Colonel Hastings and others; the farmers gathered in the library and walked behind, among whom were Allden, Tice, Hewett and the schoolmaster; there were 'others who waited at the back of the church–Shrubb, Penfold the carpenter and the Winters'.[14] So passed Richard Sumner, unsung and unremembered on any memorial.

Morton Sumner succeeded his father in possession of the Priory estate, but only for a year. He died of smallpox in London in 1874 and the property passed to his sister, Miss Georgiana Sumner, who died in 1904. Meanwhile, Ferdinand Smallpeice bought the reversion of the property, but did not enter into possession of the Priory House until after Miss Sumner's death.[15] However, on 14

May 1888 an Indenture signed by Charlotte Caroline Georgiana Howard of Hampton, Seale, conveyed to Mark Smallpeice the lordships of the manors of Puttenham Priory and Puttenham Bury for the sum of £500.[16] So the manorial rights of the two manors returned to Puttenham. This gave Mark Smallpeice the right to hold manorial courts and to receive all manorial dues payable by copyholders on the estate. The last of these came from the purchasers of the *Good Intent* Public House in 1925. The Priory was sold by Mr. William Smallpeice in 1933 when he removed from Guildford to the old rectory and renamed it the 'Manor House'. A new rectory had been built in 1908.

Many of the villagers have appeared in their places in this village story, the tragedies of those who were paupers have already been dealt with and the story of the Budd family, the female members of whom 'exercised their charms' and produced six bastard children between December 1813 and September 1839. Kerry, however, takes our minds off these less inspiring incidents and gives us a colourful description of the 'Perambulation of Puttenham Parish 1824', 'taken from a copy of a memorandum deposited in the Parish Chest with the churchwardens accounts'. The heading runs thus:

> Puttenham, Surrey
>
> After public notice having been given in this and the adjoining parishes. The Bounds of this aforesaid Parish were walked on the 9th day of April 1824.

57 men and boys took part 'led by Henry Long Esq.' of Hampton, Seale. They 'began in the middle of the road opposite the *Jolly Farmer,* went up Holloway Hill and onto the turnpike, here they walked in the middle of the road thereby claiming the common land along the road known as the Lints; then down the bank of the stream to Shoelands and down the middle of the lakes' (presumably by boat). At Cutt Mill corner 'seven old men here certified that they had walked to this corner (some of them twice) fifty years since'. Then follow minute details of roads, paths and fields until the procession arrived back at the *Jolly Farmer.* What refreshment they received on the way is not stated but the reason why they started and finished at the *Jolly Farmer* is obvious.[17]

Throughout the century the public spirit of the tenant farmers appears. Time after time the same names occur as churchwarden, overseer or waywarden, son following father in the families of the

Keens, the Tices, the Simmonds, the Fludders, and the Hewetts, all playing their part in the village in the 19th century. They may have formed a village oligarchy, but it was a successful form of government. At the end of the century the name of Allden of Shoelands appears as Overseer and later he held the last parish office, with the exception of churchwarden, viz. that of way-warden, in 1894. Without such men the parochial system, begun by the Tudors and continued for over 300 years, could not have operated. Throughout England yeoman farmers, such as these, carried the burden of parish administration. Their names appear in the Rate Books, in the Churchwardens' Accounts, as contributors to poor relief, and the weight of taxation fell upon them, including the liability to tithe.

Tithe had always been a vexed question and had often made relations between parson and parishioner very difficult. Many attempts had been made to deal with the problem, but not until 1841 was the matter settled. An 'Apportionment of the Rent charge in lieu of Tithes in the Parish of Puttenham in the County of Surrey' was agreed on 16 December 1840.[18] An assessment had been made in 1835, but this was not considered sufficient, so a new one was undertaken. After 'divers meetings' between the Commissioner, Joseph Townsend, and the land holders it was accepted that 1692 acres and 16 perches of land in Puttenham were subject to tithe and that commutation amounting to £365 16s. 2d. was payable to the rector in lieu of tithe. These apportionments and the tithe maps enable us to visualize the villages of England and no less can we picture Puttenham at that time. The apportionment states the 'corn yield of Puttenham as 348,54204 bushels of wheat, 618,2031 bushels of barley and 889,83838 bushels of oats, wheat being 7s. 0½, barley 3s. 11½ and oats 2s. 9 per bushel'.[19] Landowners, tenant farmers and, even, occupiers of houses and gardens are detailed; furthermore, the map itself records the names of the fields in the village and it is possible to distinguish the owner of each and to see Puttenham as an entirely agricultural community.

Churchwardens Accounts are always interesting, with their wide range of control. The early ones belonging to Puttenham have been lost; there are copies made by Kerry of the Accounts from 1718, but the original ones only begin in 1824. From these occasional glimpses the everyday life of some of the villagers appears. Mrs. Winter was paid 4s. for washing one surplice twice; one wonders whose fault it was which necessitated such an expenditure of effort. Arthur Avenell received '6d. for half a day's work clearing up leaves in the churchyard', an autumnal job which had to be done 150 years ago, as today. Richard Fludder, as Churchwarden, paid a bill for 'coles' and in 1833 45 dozen sparrow heads cost the church 15s. Dinners at the *King Arms,* on the Hog's Back, appear in several entries: e.g. 'dinner for three 15s.' on 17 May 1831, and 'Dinner 7s. 6d.' on 1 September.[20] From these accounts we learn the names of some of the artisans in the village—Caesar, the baker; Penfold, the carpenter, a member of whose family seems to have been a carpenter in the village for several generations; Fludder, a yeoman farmer and blacksmith, and Hooker who succeeded him at the smithy. Kerry gives an account of the death of Richard Fludder, yeoman, on 14 March 1873—'the last of the Fludders of Puttenham'. His family had been there for over 200 years and they had nearly always played an important part in the life of the village. Kerry pays great tribute to him and speaks of the number of people who attended the funeral, including the squire, Mr. Morton Sumner. He also gives gruesome details of the grave digging. 'No less than five skulls were turned up at the digging of Mr. Fludder's grave, some of which, exhibited the teeth in high preservation. Amongst the remains was a breastplate with the name of Letitia Fludder, Mr. Fludder's mother'.[21]

Kerry tells us of some of the artisans. There was, he says, Cranham, the shepherd, who remembered Puttenham Fair in the early years of the century. This fair was held at the *Jolly Farmer* and the stock for sale, we are told, largely consisted of sheep, and, to Cranham's delight, the shepherds were always given a dinner at the *Jolly Farmer.* 'He thought the last sale made was of a sow and litter and this took place at the stable door'.[22] Callingham, the woodcutter, appears, and it is recorded that he was given two months hard labour for assaulting a policeman in the *Jolly Farmer* on 8 December 1877. 'The defendant appeared staggered at being sent to prison at all'.[23] We learn of the sad death of William Birkhead, butler to Mr. Sumner, who fell down the steps outside the Priory and 'was found to be dead when he was brought into the house'.[24] The grisly story of Daniel Brown is also told. He hanged himself in the barn in the Street at 5 o'clock in the

Priory Farm House, The Street

morning–an ungodly hour to perform such a deed. Kerry continues: 'Deceased was not a man of temperate habits, and his being out of employment was supposed to have caused mental depression under which he committed the unfortunate act'.[25] The rumour went round that 'Old Master Budd', a retired butcher, was dead. Kerry called at his house and found him making his morning cup of tea. Much relieved Kerry went on his way and saw Penfold, the carpenter, coming to meet him. Penfold told him that Budd was dead. 'Nonsense' said Kerry 'he is cooking his breakfast'. Penfold turned and 'disappeared quickly round the corner and out of sight'. Penfold was the village coffin maker and he realised that business had not come his way that morning![26] Even the rector, the Revd. Charles Duckworth, was not free from Kerry's reminiscences. 'He went on horseback to visit parishioners at Joy's Lodge, on the Hog's Back. Riding his horse through the garden he suddenly felt the animal's back legs sink and found himself and his horse astride a baulk of timber, which lay across the cesspool! This had been covered with branches and the pit was not visible. Mercifully, help was near and horse and rider were rescued, only the horse's hind quarters penetrated the cesspool'.[27] Kerry's anecdotes are numerous, but village amusements have their humorous side as well.

In the middle of the 19th century entertainment or any intellectual exercise had to be found in the village. Communication with Guildford was by carriage, waggon or on foot, consequently the villagers were quite content with what the parish could provide. Cricket matches were arranged with neighbouring clubs and occasionally the results were unorthodox. The *Surrey Advertiser* for 22 May 1869 reports a cricket match which seems to have been a little out of the ordinary. On 14 May at Puttenham, in a match between Pirbright and Puttenham, the home umpire gave a decision of 'run out'. Pirbright objected and asked the umpire to leave the field. This he refused to do, so he was removed bodily![28] Another form of entertainment seems to have been an organization known as 'The Old Club' and in June 1869 it appears to have have had a busy day. It was the anniversary of the club and the members formed a procession, probably in the Street, and led by the Guildford band they marched to the rectory. There they were met by the Revd. Charles Duckworth and his curate, the Revd. Charles Kerry. The two clerics were escorted to the church, where a service was held and a sermon was preached, whether by Duckworth or Kerry is not stated. After the service all the members went to the *Jolly Farmer* for 'a first class dinner'. From there they proceeded to the Priory 'to see Mr. Sumner', (with our knowledge of Mr. Sumner he was probably not too pleased to see them). Then they marched back to the rectory for dancing on the lawn and for amusement on a large steam roundabout. The excitement was further increased by the arrival of some gipsies, who were on their way to Ascot.[29] Unfortunately there is no indication as to what the 'Old Club' was nor who belonged to it, but obviously the anniversary was a great occasion.

More intellectual entertainment is reported in the issue of the *Surrey Advertiser* for 11 December 1869, when a lecture was given in Puttenham. The account states that 'a pleasant and instructive evening was spent by a number of parishioners in Puttenham on Tuesday evening in the National School Room when E.S. Curry Esq. of Lewes gave a lecture on "The Air we Breathe", ... we hope this will stimulate other lecturers to come forward either with lectures or readings, which, if interspersed with music would serve to make some winter evenings positively enjoyable'.[30] The Revd. Charles Kerry, curate and antiquarian, was obviously persuaded to respond to this suggestion, probably without music, when he gave two lectures in the schoolroom, one on archaeological finds he had made in Puttenham and another on Waverley Abbey. A less intellectual entertainment was held when Miss Perrett arranged a musical evening at the school, the first part consisting of secular and the second of sacred music; the proceeds to be given to the Puttenham National School.[31] Thus, in spite of apparent isolation villagers in rural communities all over the country were able to supply their own means of relaxation.

In July 1858 there must have been great excitement in Puttenham, as the rumour was abroad that Queen Victoria was to visit the village. Because of an outbreak of cholera at Aldershot it was considered wise for the Queen to hold her review of her troops away from the camp. Puttenham Heath was selected. The Queen stood on Frosbury Hill and took the salute. Afterwards a memorial stone was placed on the hill to mark the occasion. It consisted of a flat stone in the centre of which was placed a flag pole. This was blown down in 1869, but some restoration was carried out in 1953 to commemorate the accession of her great-great-grand-daughter, Elizabeth II.

Until the middle of the century the village governed itself in nearly all branches of administration, but by the 1860s the central organization was gaining control and old ways had to give way to new. This appears clearly in the case of the House of Industry at Ash to which Puttenham had sent its paupers since 1797. An Act of Parliament was passed in 1868 dissolving all Gilbert Unions and, as a result, Puttenham was incorporated in the Guildford Union in 1869. Mr. James Hewett, farmer of Priory Farm House, was elected as Guardian to represent Puttenham on the Guildford Board of Guardians.[32] In 1874 the Ash House of Industry was sold by the Farnham Union and an order was issued by the Guildford Guardians directing Farnham to pay Puttenham its share of the sale, amounting to £174 8s. 2d. Pauper conditions at Guildford were certainly better than at Ash, as a result of the work of Mr. Hewett and when he died the village lost a champion of its rights. In March 1885 the *Surrey Advertiser* gave a description of his funeral: 'The mournful procession left the church and wended its way to the last resting place', (the cemetery) 'the snow, which was falling somewhat heavily covered the ground with a pall of virgin whiteness'. A typical piece of 19th century reporting.[33]

The cemetery was a new addition to Puttenham, but the scheme could no longer be a purely parochial one, for the central authority had now to be consulted. The Vestry approached the Local Government Board for permission to sell some parish lands to meet the expense of acquiring a cemetery. In July 1881 the Board gave permission for the sale and in August 1882 the same Board allowed that the £68 6s. 2d. resulting from the sale, should be used for the cemetery at Puttenham.[34] The independence of the village was passing rapidly. The last vestiges disappeared when Mr. Allden was 'elected waywarden, only until the new local Government Act of 1894 should come into force'[35]; and when the oligarchy of the Vestry was ended by the establishment of the Parish Council. During the centuries the Vestry had dealt with all manner of problems—relief of the poor, roads, vermin, etc., as well as church matters. Gradually, however, its powers were taken over by the central authority and its concern with church matters was assumed by the Parochial Church Council established in 1921 as a result of the Parochial Church Councils (Powers) Act, 1921. All that now remains to the Vestry is the election of churchwardens. 'However, there is some pleasure for the historically minded parishioners in sharing the proceedings of a democratic governing body whose story in England is at least six hundred years old'.[36] The uneventful story of Puttenham in the 19th century of its squires, its tenant farmers, its villagers and its amusements can be matched in any English village of the period.

NOTES

1. Kerry, vol.vi, p.106.
2. Guildford Muniment Room, 5/6/54.
3. Kerry, vol.x, p.249.
4. National Society Record, 1829.
5. Vestry Minute Books 1882-1919: Guildford Muniment Room PSH/Put/8/27.
6. School Log Book, 1893-1921.
7. Ibid.
8. Ibid.
9. Terrier of Puttenham 1765 in the possession of the Lord of the Manor.
10. Sale particulars quoted by G.B. Gosling in 'Notes on Puttenham', fol.110.
11. *D.N.B.*, vol.xii, p.232 and R.G. Vevers in 'Papers Read to the Puttenham and Wanborough History Society' 1967-1969.
12. Surrey Archaeological Collections, vol.xliv, p.82.
13. Kerry, vol.vi, p.126.
14. Kerry, vol.vii, pp.117-119.
15. G.B. Gosling, 'Notes on Puttenham', fol.7.
16. Indentures in possession of the Puttenham and Wanborough History Society.
17. Kerry, vol.ii, p.151.
18. Tithe Map and Apportionment–Guildford Muniment Room, PSH/Put/13/1.
19. The figures representing the corn yield are misleading. The commas indicate decimal points–thus 348.5 bushels of wheat, 618.2 bushels of barley and 889.8 bushels of oats. The returns had by law to be made in bushels, because the price of corn was fixed per bushel, and the figures after the decimal points represent the odd pecks or gallons. These bushels are the amount of tithe due to the tithe-owner–in this case the rector. They do not relate to the real or supposed total yield of grain in the parish.
20. Churchwardens' Accounts of the Parish of Puttenham: Guildford Muniment Room, PSH/Put/8/1.
21. Kerry, vol.vi, p.149.
22. Ibid., p.61.

23. *Surrey Advertiser,* 8 December, 1877.
24. Kerry, Vol.viii, p.85.
25. Ibid., vol.ii, p.247.
26. Ibid., vol.viii, pp.120-123.
27. Ibid., vol.viii, p.132.
28. *Surrey Advertiser,* 22 May, 1869.
29. *Surrey Advertiser,* 12 June, 1869.
30. *Surrey Advertiser,* 11 December, 1869.
31. From information given by Mr. Tice of Runfold.
32. *Surrey Advertiser,* 12 June, 1869.
33. *Surrey Advertiser,* 7 March, 1885.
34. Kingston Record Office, BG6/11/20.
35. Churchwardens' Accounts: Guildford Muniment Room, PSH/Put/8/27.
36. W.E. Tate, *The Parish Chest,* p.25.

EPILOGUE

THE TWENTIETH CENTURY

LOOKING BACK to the first few years of the 20th century the picture of the village seems to have changed little from that of a hundred years before and it reveals a world which has only a small connection with ours today. Certain changes had taken place, however. The lord of the manor, Mr. Ferdinand Smallpeice, did not live in the Priory as other lords of the manor had done; he lived in Guildford and let the Priory house. A new school had been built in 1904 and a new rectory in 1908. The old rectory was let until Mr. William Smallpeice took up residence there in 1933 and renamed it the Manor House. Thus there were alterations in landmarks hitherto accepted as permanent. In the village, life was still centred round agriculture, and the commuter had hardly appeared. Except for rather primitive binders, farming was not mechanized. Transport of farm produce was entirely by horse and waggon. Hops were delivered to the breweries in Guildford or to the Borough in London and vegetables were supplied to the Royal Surrey Hospital, to Charterhouse and to King Edward's School at Witley.

It is interesting to learn of their lives from those who were engaged in agriculture during the early years of the century. The hurdle-maker, George Turvil, who brought up a family of ten children in a 'two-up and two-down' cottage, was considered to be earning a good wage when he took home about £1 a week, but he had to work hard for it! His hurdles were greatly needed on the farms, not only in Puttenham, and he would walk to Normandy, Wanborough, Compton or Elstead to make them on the spot. The farmer cut chestnut and hazel saplings between 1 October and 25 March and then in April the hurdle-maker came carrying his tools. These would include two axes, a bill-hook, a clasp knife and the block on which to build the hurdles, which alone weighed between

20 and 30 pounds. He set to work immediately and was paid a piece-work rate on the basis of 3s. 6d. for a dozen hurdles. The work usually lasted until July, after which he would help with sheep shearing or potato digging. He was an expert at shearing sheep and often walked as far as Pirbright, about seven miles, to help the shepherd there. In spite of hard work he lived to the age of 91.[1]

The Shepherd was another dedicated figure. For 11 months of the year he was responsible for a flock of, perhaps, 500 sheep. These had to be moved regularly from one field to another to ensure that they were on good clean pasture. Each field was divided into sections by hurdles and the sheep were penned into these divisions in turn to prevent indiscriminate feeding. Lambing was a time of great responsibility for the shepherd. Then he lived in a small wheeled hut near the ewes so as to be ready for any emergency; now ewes in lamb are brought under cover for lambing. When the sheep were ready for market he had to drive them along the roads to Farnham or Guildford, an unthinkable task today with the traffic hurtling along on the Hog's Back. His wages were small—15s. a week—and yet the sheep farmer depended entirely on his skill.[2]

The carter, Stenning, was the aristocrat among the agricultural labourers. Like the shepherd his smock denoted his position. He was an early riser; his team had to be fed, watered and dressed before 7 a.m. when he took it out for the day's work, be it cultivations or drawing the farm waggons. The carter was proud of his horses and those who can remember the superb Suffolk punches and shire horses will readily understand how much they meant to him. When World War I broke out horses were commandeered from every part of the country for service with the army and it was with heavy hearts that the carters saw them go. A carter in a neighbouring village tells how he was warned that army representatives were in the neighbourhood. Accordingly, he took his horses into a spinney and tied them up. Two he left in their stalls, knowing that he would be allowed to keep them in order to work the farm. He remembered to remove all the harness belonging to the animals he had hidden, so as not to raise the suspicion of the military visitors. By this ruse he saved his horses. Few, if any, hurdle-makers or carters can be found in our villages today, although shepherds are still needed, especially on the moors or the fells.

The life of the women was hard, with little recreation. There were often six or seven children in a family and they had to be clothed and fed on a very small budget and cared for often in a 'two-up and two-down' house. Water had to be carried from a well, which was shared with others. Wood was the chief fuel and this had to be collected from the lanes or hedges to supplement the faggots which could be bought. Cooking was done on ranges which had to be blackleaded, a task usually reserved for Saturday morning. To help the family income the mothers worked in the fields, took in washing, or went out charring. A strict rule was observed in many households that there should be as little work as possible done on Sundays and this was a relief to the overworked mother of the family. The majority of families went to church and the children also went to Sunday School in the afternoon.[3] For the boys there was always work to be found on the farms, although an increasing number left the village for the town as apprentices or shop assistants. For the girls there was little else than domestic service. To get into a good family was their aim, even if it meant carrying coals, preparing vegetables, or filling hip baths for the gentry from heavy copper jugs. In service in the big houses they were fed well, they had companionship and they learnt the art of housewifery, which would later be useful in their own homes.

Until 1915, when he retired, the Revd. George Clarke and his wife walked tirelessly round the village visiting their parishioners. The rector is remembered by some today as a tall figure with a white beard and wearing a black frock-coat. He was known as 'Daddy Clarke'. He had been largely responsible for building the school and still kept his interest in it by teaching there for an hour every day. Mrs. Clarke took the needlework classes for the younger children and held the Mothers' Meeting and the Girls' Friendly Society in the rectory. The daughters of Canon Yarborough, who became rector in 1918, continued the work of the Clarkes in the village and even taught dancing and held sing-songs in the church room. Worthy members of the parish organized the Boot Club, the Clothing Club and the Coal Club. The village nurse was always at the beck and call of the harassed mother or the woman approaching confinement. There are many stories of her willing answer to emergency appeals. Several villagers today remember the miles she walked or bicycled to bring help in distress.

Before 1914 there was still an atmosphere of manorial benevolence in Puttenham. The Countess of Visconti, who was the tenant of the Priory, showed concern that some of the school children were unable to get to their homes for dinner and return in time for afternoon school. She, therefore, ordered that vegetables from the Priory garden, together with a sheep's head and bones, should be sent once a week to the Coffee House, now Keston Cottage, and here they were made into soup by Miss Harcourt's grandmother. The children could then obtain a hot and nourishing meal to supplement their sandwiches. These facts show that every effort was made to help or entertain the people of Puttenham, even though this way would not be acceptable today.

Until World War I the villagers accepted the pattern of their lives as it had been for the last hundred years. They were unaware of any approaching change. They still claimed their common rights. The village Pound on Puttenham Heath was in use in the early years of the 20th century; the dues were paid to the lord of the manor by farmers whose cattle had strayed and were impounded. The agricultural labourer quite happily held his cottage on a 'monthly hiring'. At a Parish Meeting held on 24 October 1895 great indignation was expressed because the lord of the manor had filled in the pond at the top of the Street. Further, he had given permission to the newly-formed golf club to occupy land which carried the right of grazing, turf cutting and wooding of the copyholders in Puttenham. At this meeting Mr. Callingham was angry over the infringement of his rights on the Heath. He demanded that 'the depradations of the golf club' should be stopped. 'He paid his rent to the lord of the manor', he said, and 'if he died to-morrow the Manor would mark his best horse, but would not subscribe to another'. He was 'going to stop the power of the golf club'. Continuing, Mr. Callingham wanted to know on whose authority had the lord of the manor enclosed the pond at the top of the Street and asked that it should be re-opened. Mr. Callingham was unable to gain his points since the chairman ruled that the Parish Council was not competent to deal with either matter.[4]

The Pound, which was on Puttenham Heath near the Golf Club, caused considerable correspondence between the clerk to the

The Forge, The Street

Parish Council and the lord of the manor. The clerk, George Honey, wrote to Mr. Mark Smallpeice in 1897 asking for permission to enlarge the Pound by four feet at either end and to 'make the pound more suitable for the purposes required'. Mr. Smallpeice agreed. In 1898 the clerk wrote again to enquire from Mr. Smallpeice as to whether he intended to claim the poundage on animals placed in it. The lord of the manor replied that he did so intend.[5] He was, of course, within his rights, as poundage was a manorial due. There were further letters which indicate that the Pound was enlarged and used, but after 1908 there is no mention of it.

The agricultural cottages seem to us to have been held on a precarious lease—in general this was a 'monthly hiring' and on a basis of 2s. a week. Even the school was a '½ yearly hiring' from 'the land lady', Miss Sumner, the daughter of Richard Sumner of the Priory. In 1902 'A Block of 6 Freehold Cottages' in the Street (now 77 to 81) was offered for sale. The particulars gave the information that the cottages 'share a well, bakehouse, washhouse, and closet'. These cottages were on a 'weekly hiring'.[6] This insecurity does not appear to have worried the tenants who occupied them.

An institution which would not be tolerated in a village today was the slaughter house in Puttenham Street. In 1906 Joseph Pope was in correspondence with Mr. Ferdinand Smallpeice, the lord of the manor, on the question of rent for 'cottage, slaughter house, stable, coach-house and field'. After some haggling it was agreed that Joseph Pope should rent all these premises for £30 per annum. In his letter Pope refers to the slaughter house as though there had been one there before.[7] In all probability there had been, as most villages of any size possessed one.

Street lighting had been a problem since the question first came before the Vestry in 1881. Donations were eventually obtained and street lamps were erected. In those days, however, they were gas lamps and had to be individually lit every night. For some time a lamp-lighter could not be found, but at last, at a Lighting Committee Meeting held on 18 September 1911 Mr. G. Grey was engaged at a wage of £10 2s. 4d. per annum 'to light the lamps as per specification and allow 2s. 6d. for cleaning the lamps before lighting'. At the same time 'Tender for painting was received from Mr. A.S. Jeal for the sum of Eighteen Shillings to paint the

12 Lamps as per Specification'. This tender was also accepted.[8] Already, on 30 March 1910 Jeal had been paid 2s. 3d. for 'Mending Lamps' and G. Grey £8 19s. 0d. for 'Lighting Lamps',[9] and on 31 March 1911 Jeal was paid 7s. 6d. for 'Repairs to St. Lamps' and Grey £9 8s. 6d. for 'Lighting Village Lamps'.[10] This was all before the tenders accepted by the Lighting Committee on 18 September 1911. It is interesting to note that the first payments thereafter, on 28 March and 30 March respectively were to Jeal for 'Painting & Mending St. Lamps' £1 0s. 9d. and to Grey for 'Lighting Village Lamps' £10 5s. 9d.[11] Evidently both men had had a rise in wages within 12 months of their tenders being accepted. The lamps remained until World War II when, because of 'Black-out' regulations, they were taken out of use.

The village as it is remembered by those who lived in it before 1920, was a small almost self-contained community, whose chief concern was still agriculture. When the War of 1914 broke out Puttenham, in company with all other villages in England, rose to the occasion. Belgian refugees were billeted and fed and the children were received in the village school. First-aid classes were held and afternoons for bandage-making were organized. Food was short and Mrs. Mowbray Howard of Seale with Mrs. A.C. Tuckwell of Puttenham arranged for meals to be cooked and served to the children. Meanwhile there was anxiety in many homes for the 18 or more young men who had joined the forces. On 3 October 1920 a War Memorial was unveiled by the Earl of Midleton to the memory of those 13 who did not return. This was erected outside the church.

Some of the villagers still remember extremes of weather. On Thursday, 2 August 1906, there was a terrible thunderstorm in Guildford when wind and hail caused fearful damage. Puttenham, sheltered by the Hog's Back, did not suffer so badly as Guildford, Shalford and other places, but the fury of the wind and the lashing rain is still remembered today. *The Surrey Advertiser* reported that 'havoc was wrought on the Hog's Back ... and the engineering staff was engaged all night in clearing the wreckage of the telephone wires on the road'.[12] Another remembrance is of a very bad winter 'sometime before the war' when 'the plough-boys got frozen ears' and 'after rubbing themselves with tallow' were sewn into flannel shirts! Again, the winter of 1916 is recalled, when there were 'walls of ice' on the Hog's Back, 'three weeks skating at Cutt Mill and the congregation arriving at the church on sledges', the snow making any other way of transport impossible. The winter of 1963 was terribly severe, but it was far easier for the villagers to keep warm in that year. There was by that time central heating in many homes and gas or electric fires in the majority of houses.

The end of World War I in 1918 saw changes for the better in the village. The motor car was coming into use and motor buses, heralded by the 'No.31' on the Hog's Back in 1920, made communications with Guildford and Farnham much easier. The men could get to football matches in either town and the women no longer had to walk to do their shopping there. The latter were offered some relaxation in the Women's Institute, which was started in Puttenham in 1920. In a vain hope that it might help to prevent another war the Women's Institute became a 'Corporate Associate' of the League of Nations Union in 1924.[13] The old order was passing and the end of the manorial system was in sight. This came about when the lord of the manor received the last dues for which he had any right from the *Good Intent* Public House, in the Street. On 17 December 1926, Mr. F.C. Potter, a trustee for the shareholders, took over the *Good Intent,* the property of F.A. Crooke & Co. Ltd. The dues payable to the lord of the manor were:

Fine	£108 12s. 0d.
Quit rent	10s. 0d.
Heriot	£ 20 14s. 0d.

Together with admission fees and extinguishment charges the total was £199 18s. 6d.[14] By an Act of Parliament in 1925 all manorial dues were abolished[15] and the title of lord of the manor from that date has had little but archaic significance.

The years between 1930 and 1970 are sharply divided by the second World War. Life before the war was not vastly different from what it was at the beginning of the century. The church services, especially Mattins, were well attended and the social divisions, which were still clearly cut were expressed by the difference in the congregation which went to Mattins from that which attended Evensong. The school was still run on simple lines and as the Marwick Hall had not yet been built, it was taught in somewhat cramped conditions in the school classrooms. Farming was only slowly becoming mechanized; the number of agricultural workers was not greatly reduced and wages were low—a different world from 1970.

In 1933 Mr. Smallpeice, who had been a non-resident lord of the manor, came to live at 'The Grange', formerly the rectory, which he re-named 'The Manor House'. From here he managed his manorial estate and farmed his own lands. Mrs. Smallpeice interested herself in all the village activities. She became President of the Puttenham branch of the Women's Institute and opened her grounds for charity sales of work or garden parties.

By 1930 transport to Guildford or Farnham had become easier. Shoppers could go to Guildford by pony trap or by car at a charge of 6d. per head. The motor car was not as rapid a mode of travelling as it might have been. It found hills somewhat of a problem; in fact it discovered it was easier to negotiate one by going up backwards. On Oliver Hill it went forward as far as the entrance to Holloway Vere, there it turned and finished the ascent to the Hog's Back in reverse! The pony trap was more reliable, for it went straight ahead to Guildford. In 1927 the 'Brownie Bus' began running and continued to do so until its driver had an accident and was killed. The 'Yellow Bus' then appeared, in 1929, and plied between Guildford and Farnham until it was merged with the 'Aldershot and District Traction Company', which had started serving the route in 1930. After the war the number of cars increased rapidly, so a bus service was not such a vital necessity as it had been. Nevertheless hourly buses through the village have continued until 1971.

Recreation for the villagers was found in certain annual events. The Flower Show was held in July. This was considered of sufficient importance to warrant closing the school for the day to allow the children to take part. There were not only exhibits of flowers, vegetables and children's arrangements, but there were roundabouts, swings, bowling for the pig, coconut shies, races for children and adults and a tug-of-war between Puttenham and Wanborough. All the events were carried out to the strains of the Elstead Band. It was a great day for everyone. There were other excitements, if less ambitious ones, such as the Sunday School party at the Rectory; country dancing; acting and poetry recitations by the Girls' Friendly Society, which were given in the grounds at Berthorpe; and concerts organized by the Girl Guides

The Cutt Mill road, 1930

to raise money to enable the troop to go to camp. This camping holiday was a highlight for those who took part and they still remember the sing-songs around the camp fire. There were, also, monthly dances, or entertainments, given by the Young Conservatives, the Imps, which were very popular.

Two annual events which were of great importance were Empire Day, when there were marches through the village, the waving of flags and the singing of 'Land of Hope and Glory', and the ceremony of 'Beating the Bounds' at Rogationtide. This latter was discontinued during the war, but was renewed in 1964. Thus during the years 1930-39 life in Puttenham continued in an uneventful and parochial manner, hardly perturbed by the financial troubles in the world outside during the early '30s and not over-worried by the political situation in Western Europe. Then the storm broke and the village, like all others in England, woke to the demands of war.

When war was declared in September 1939 life in Puttenham was completely changed. Civil Defence, the Home Guard and a branch of the Red Cross were quickly organized. The young men went into the fighting forces. Some of the younger women entered the different branches of the women's services and others worked in the factories, on the buses and in canteens. The older women, or those who had young children, went to knitting afternoons at the Priory or to 'Sewing Bees' at the Manor House. Fêtes in aid of the Red Cross and St. John's Ambulance were held in the Priory Gardens. National Savings Collections were made and Red Cross lectures were given in the Old School Room, which served as the village hall. One activity which everyone remembers is the sale of 'Rural Pies'. These were pies which were delivered to the village once a week. Each person was allowed to buy one and, moreover, without coupons. The pies might not be to our satisfaction today, but during the war they were a godsend to the housewife, who often found it difficult to feed her family. They were known as 'Mr. Telfer's Ticky Snacks' and were sold in aid of the Red Cross. When the bombing of London became heavy Puttenham contributed further to the war effort by receiving evacuees. A number of them remained in the village for upwards of two years.

In spite of its rural position the village was not left unattended by Hitler's aircraft. One night incendiary bombs were dropped in the Priory Gardens. They looked like 'stars in the sky as they fell', said one observer. Lady Harcourt was dining at the time. She was in evening dress (for she still kept up the style of gracious living). Holding over her head her umbrella, as it was a wet night, she went out with her butler to inspect the bombs, which were now hanging in the trees. The butler was detailed to put them out. He wisely called on the Home Guard, some of whom were in the *Good Intent,* and it dealt successfully with the situation. Puttenham Common was set on fire in the summer of 1942, when German pilots tried to demolish the search-light at Cutt Mill. The villagers remember how the Common burned for two days. Only the search-light crew were available to deal with the fire. They worked for 36 hours without a break and they were fed by the women of the village, who brought them sandwiches and tea at intervals. The crackle of burning scrub, gorse and heather was heard all over the village. Except for one incendiary bomb, which fell on Heath Cottage, this was the extent of the damage suffered by the village.

However, every preparation was made in case of emergencies. The Fire Guard established their headquarters in the Old School Room. Here they carried out regular drill, but they were never called out. The Air-raid Wardens used a room in the new school. This was manned day and night and a special system of telephone warnings was drawn up. The Home Guard was stationed on the Hog's Back where the men were taught the use of firearms during their regular meetings. Special arrangements were made in case of casualties from enemy attack. A certain number of cottages were put ready for immediate emergency, beds, dressings and first-aid facilities being organized in each of them. Mercifully they were never required.

A certain amount of vehicle repair was done in Puttenham. The verges on the Hog's Back were used by the Canadians for tank maintenance and Venzer's Yard, which had once been a farm-yard, now became a repair depot for agricultural machinery under the War Agricultural Committee. In spite of what, with hind-sight, may seem to have been a fearful expenditure of needless effort, Puttenham gave what it could to the war effort, including the lives of those 12 young men whose names have been added to the War Memorial outside the church.

Gradually, during the years that followed, the villagers forgot the problems and difficulties which had beset them during war time. Parochial life began again, although there could never be a return to the quiet isolation of pre-war days. The great excitement at the end of the '50s was the building of the Marwick Hall. This was a tremendous effort and money was raised in various ways—dances, jumble sales, cricket matches, carnival fêtes, a mile of coins, covenants and subscriptions. It was a great day when the Marwick Hall was opened in December 1959. The cost was £4,700, but the hall was to be an invaluable asset to the village. The site had been given by Miss Jean Marwick and her generosity is remembered in the name given to the hall.

The activities which take place today, generally in the Marwick Hall, show the strong community spirit that exists in the village. This spirit is indicated by the tremendous and successful effort made in winning the 'Best Kept Village' competition in 1966, 1967 and 1968 and the 'Best Kept Village Hall' competition in 1968 and 1969. Both these competitions are organized by the Surrey Council of Social Service. The activities of Puttenham include a branch of the Women's Institute, the Mothers' Union, the Garden Club, the British Legion, lectures given under the auspices of the Workers' Educational Association, the History Society, Guides and Brownies. These are typical of village life today and they are in sharp contrast to the village concerts, the band practices, the clothing club and the shoe club which formed the chief excitements of 60 years ago. A complete revolution in all branches of life had taken place between 1910 and 1970 and this fact will be seen more clearly when we look at the church, the school and farming life over these years.

In 1930 the church had changed little since the beginning of the century, except for the setting up of Parochial Church Councils under the Parochial Church Councils (Powers) Act of 1921 instead of church government by the rector and the Vestry. *The London Gazette* of 3 July 1931, however, forecast addition to the work of the rector of Puttenham. *The Gazette* stated that after due consideration the bishop of Guildford and the Parochial Church Councils of Puttenham and Wanborough had decided to ask the Privy Council to recommend to the King that these two parishes should be united under the Union of Benefices Measure 1923. King George V gave his consent, opposition by the Revd. John Pearce was over-ruled and it was agreed that when the benefice of Wanborough fell vacant the union should take place. This was effected in 1946, when the Revd. John Pearce of Wanborough resigned. The two parishes now form a united benefice, but each has its own Parochial Church Council.

Meanwhile there have been alterations in the church services during the 1960s. The experimental liturgy, "Second Series", has been introduced and the Family Communion service has taken pride of place over Mattins. A choir has also been re-introduced. We last looked at the furnishings of the church at the 'restoration' of 1861. Since then further alterations have been carried out. The organ was placed in the south transept in 1951 and new pews and a new pulpit have been installed since 1930. The Victorian tiles on the floor of the nave have been replaced by York stone to celebrate the 800th anniversary of the foundation of the church of St. John the Baptist and in 1971 oil-fired heaters were substituted for the coke boiler. In spite of changes in liturgy, worship and furnishings the church still holds its place among the people and it continues to dominate the village with its massive tower, as it has done for nearly 500 years.

The School also has changed immeasurably for the better. The School Log Book 1921 shows that during the years 1921 to 1939 the school had not moved far beyond the ideas of the late 19th century, when educational work was not high on the list of priorities. There are entries during the '20s which indicate that the school was not up to standard. In 1924 an Inspector's report states that 'the school cannot be said to be as satisfactory as it should be'. Again 'the Teacher of needlework appears to know very little about her subject'. However, in 1922 the Headmaster had received commendation from the visiting inspector, who stated that he 'deserves credit for his sound gardening instruction'! Many entries point to the fact that the agricultural needs of the village were not forgotten by the school authorities as the following extracts show: 7 August 1922, 'I am instructed to keep open the school for another week on account of the late hop-picking'; 31 August 1934, 'Closed the School today for hop-picking'; 19 October 1942, 'Broke up for Potato picking holidays'.

By the end of the 1930s the School seems to have come nearer to what we would expect today. An Inspector reported that there had been 'a steady improvement in the school'. Outside events took place such as swimming classes held for boys and girls at Cutt Mill and a visit to the Aldershot Tattoo was organized in 1937. Medical services have also shown improvement; in 1933 dental inspection was introduced, in 1938 immunisation against diphtheria was carried out, and, much later, in 1962 a child-guidance psychiatrist visited the school.

The war years were difficult since some of the class rooms were commandeered for Air-raid Wardens or were used for making black-out curtains. Those rooms which were still available for teaching had a sombre and depressing atmosphere, due to the fact that the windows were covered with protective netting. Staff shortage was a problem as, even when married teachers were appointed, they wanted time off from school when their husbands came home on leave. Fuel was difficult to obtain and an entry for January 1945 shows how desperate the situation was, 'severe winter weather and severe frost made attendance small' and 'the class rooms were very cold'. Another entry states 'bread, cheese and jam were issued for lunch' as the boiler had burst and it was not possible to cook. In April 1945 it was resolved that the official name of the school should be 'Puttenham Church of England Primary School (mixed and infants)'. As such the school is now recognized as one of the best in the county of Surrey.

When the Marwick Hall was opened in 1959 it was rented for certain hours by the Surrey Education Committee so that the School is now able to use it for classes and for school lunches which is a great help towards the development of the curriculum; a swimming pool was opened in May 1967 and plans are on foot in 1971 to build a special craft room in which art, music and drama could be taught. There are five fully qualified teachers, including the Headmistress, and the lessons taught are on a wide range of subjects aided by B.B.C. radio and television, tape-recorders, films and gramophone records. A wide gap is evident between the subjects taught today and the three Rs, plus a little gardening and some needlework, which were the most that any pupils could learn 60 years ago. From Puttenham school the children are selected for Grammar or for Secondary Schools. Thus, instead of leaving at 12 years of age, as they did in the early years of the century, there is a way open for boys and girls to go to Technical Colleges or Universities if they can make the grade. Varied and good lunches are brought in heated vans and served to the children at the cost of 9p per day. How different from the time, at the end of the last century, when the Headmaster ordered hooks to be put in the coal house on which the children could hang the packages of sandwiches, which they had brought to school for their lunch.[16]

Perhaps farming expresses more clearly than in any other way the changes which have taken place during the last 50 years. Horses have disappeared and tractors have taken their place. Mechanization and specialization have been employed throughout the country and Puttenham is no exception to this. The man with the sickle of 150 years ago is no longer seen. He could cut, at the most, half an acre a day. Then the corn had to be tied, stooked, left to dry, carted, stacked and, later, threshed. Now the great combine harvester cuts three to four acres an hour and carries out all the stages in one process. In Puttenham the latest and largest combine which was introduced in 1970 is known as the 'Red Dragon'. The great machine fills the narrow village Street as it goes from one field to another. Potato harvesters, sprayers, balers of the latest kind can now be seen working in the fields. The time when 50 or 60 men would be working together lifting potatoes with forks is forgotten and so are the days when women gleaned. Tractors and large trailers are to be seen everywhere and the waggon is a thing of the past.

This mechanization of farming has ended the day of the small farmer. In the 19th century farming in the village was in the hands of tenant farmers almost entirely. By the 1930s their lands were being absorbed by the bigger farms. This is largely the result of the capital requirements of modern agriculture. It is reckoned today that the investment rate in a farm of two hundred acres may involve £50,000 in the land and farm buildings and £12,000 in livestock, machinery and crops. No wonder that the Tofts, the Fludders, the Tices, the Simmonds and other yeomen farmers of 80 to 100 years ago have disappeared and that two or three farmers between them now farm the lands of Puttenham.

In spite of the changes in farming, the preservation of the countryside is something that is not forgotten by the large farmers, although economic considerations must take first place. The removal of hedges is a necessity to provide more space in which the large machines can operate. The farmers are generally sympathetic to the anxiety of the ecologists on this score and Mr. Thornton, who owns the largest amount of land in Puttenham, has cut down only those hedges which had to be sacrificed to enable his farming policy to be followed. New farm buildings, also, can damage the beauty of a village, but again the farmers are well

Hook Lane, 1971

aware of the danger. The large new barn at Grey's Farm, Puttenham, has been discreetly hidden behind the old 18th-century one which faces the road.

In the case of hops, which had been grown by most of the tenant farmers in the 19th century, great changes have taken place. Before the second World War there were a number of hop fields in the village. Today the crop is grown by only one farmer and the amount that he may send to the Borough Market is strictly controlled. The harvesting of hops, also, has changed and has been completely modernized. Picking used to be done by gipsies, then the hops were dried in the old hop kiln in Puttenham Street by means of heat from a charcoal furnace. Today, 1970, the strands of hops are cut by hand, but the actual picking, sorting and sacking are done by machinery installed in the barn behind Dark Lane. A new dryer is now being built near the picking machines. When this is completed the old hop kilns in the Street will become redundant and will probably be converted into houses.

Thus in agriculture, as in industry, practices are continually changing, as farmers, reacting to economic demands, absorb new technology in order to improve productivity and to cut back overheads. In Surrey there are heavy land requirements today and there may well be more in the future, necessitating further intensification, specialization and mechanization. The villagers cannot but be aware of what may happen in Puttenham. Nevertheless, there is much in the village to remind us of the past in the domestic and farm buildings which still remain. These are documents in stone and act as mirrors of its history through the centuries.

The oldest houses in Puttenham are Winter's Farm, Rosemary Cottage and the Old Cottage. These are all 15th-century buildings, which are timber framed and were built, in all probability by one man, the village housewright of the moment, and were designed on the open hall plan. These houses are clear evidence of the tenant farmers in the 15th century, who, breaking away from the restrictive conditions of the manorial system of farming, were anxious to express their new-found freedom in building houses that would give them more of the comforts of life, as they saw them. The houses were built in the Street close to each other, since the owners had small farms on the outskirts of the village, and the farmers needed to be near their neighbours in order 'to share their limited capital equipment (especially the eight-ox plough)'.[17]

The comparatively large number of 16th-century houses which still stand in the Street are an indication of the increasing wealth of the Tudor period. It was an age of excitement and experiment. This appears in the changes which can be seen in the buildings and the new architectural devices employed, such as the second floor which was built over the hall, the outside chimney added to a wall of the house and the jetty erected to carry the upper storey. These examples of Tudor domestic architecture can be seen at Street Farm, Farm Cottage or Hook Lane Cottages. The housewright was obviously kept busy in the village at this time. It was his heyday, but when bricks superseded wood in the 17th century his work was gradually undertaken by the architect and the bricklayer. It is probable that the prospective house builders and the housewright learned much from the derelict Waverley Abbey. Waverley was not far from Puttenham, and there can be little doubt that the villagers brought back from the ruins of the Abbey not only new ideas, but, also, materials for use in the erection of their own houses.

By the 17th century new social conditions obtained and a class of wealthy gentry appeared in the village—the Lusshers who had come to the old Priory House in the 16th century, the Leighs who had bought the house at Shoelands from Sir Nicholas Lussher and the Wyatts who had come to live at Rodsall. These families required larger houses, which would reflect their social position, which would be more commodious and which should be built in the modern building material—in brick. Therefore, it is not surprising that brick was employed as the material for the three prestige houses built in Puttenham at the beginning of the 17th century. Soon the yeomen farmers followed the example of the landed gentry and built themselves substantial small houses in the Street, such as, Jasmine and Keston Cottages, Crossways and the present School House. These farm houses and the large barns, many of which are still standing, indicate the rise in prosperity of the Tices, the Snellings, the Simmonds and others. Some of these tenant farmers decorated their houses with garnetting—the insertion of small pieces of ironstone into the mortar between the bricks; this was an ornamentation employed by the farmers who wished to emphasize their social position.

Waverley Abbey

Relations with the Continent became stronger in the first half of the 18th century and architectural designs both in France and Italy were admired by those who made the Grand Tour. As a result Palladian influences appeared in England and found their way to Puttenham. The Priory House is a perfect example of an older house having received a Palladian facade. This was the work of Thomas Parker. He wanted 'a mansion house of some proportions', as we have seen.

By the middle of the 18th century the agricultural labourers were beginning to realise their worth and so required more space and more comfort in their cottages. Terraced houses were the answer to their demands. This design saved both money and land. Two examples of terraced buildings in brick exist today in Puttenham, although they are much modernized. These are Winton Cottages which belong to the Hampton Estates. The second group, 77-81 The Street, was formed out of a terrace of six and are now the homes of commuters. From these two sets of brick cottages we can conclude that the village housewright and his vernacular architecture had now completely disappeared. In the 19th century the houses of the agricultural worker became more stereotyped. Mercifully Puttenham was still too rural to suffer from this kind of building.

One moment of pure English elegance can be found in the Regency architecture of the early 19th century. France at this time was involved in war with all Europe, so no continental influence on English building was possible. Hence Regency architecture is English and it is, also, romantic, elegant and balanced. It is pleasing that Puttenham was not deprived of examples of this type of building. Heath Cottage possesses the symmetry of the period, which can be seen in its central door with sash windows each side of it, in the fanlight over the door and the wrought iron archway at the gate. This last is covered with cut yew, thereby giving the house its romantic touch. The Manor House, built as the rectory in 1824, is another example of the Regency ideal combining romanticism with beauty. Houses such as these suggest that, in spite of its deep involvement in agriculture, Puttenham was not entirely isolated from contemporary culture. The decadence in architectural design of the later 19th century is not greatly in evidence in the village, but a successful farmer, Hewett, could not forego the pleasure of being up-to-date. In 1872 he built 'Hillside', a huge example of Victorian vernacular architecture, situated in the Street.

Some of the houses built in the village in the 20th century illustrate the new social order which had entered the village. The majority of them are architect-designed and were the homes of the retired professional and the wealthy commuter. Such houses are 'Greys' (once the residence of Admiral Jellicoe) and 'Berthorpe'. They with several others, including 'Hurlands', designed by Norman Shaw, are large and gracious and express the wealth of the Edwardian era. In 1950 some delightful Council Houses were erected in the Street. These won prizes for their charm and for the way they fit in with the older houses in the village. They are an indication that even with the pressures after World War II the people of Puttenham were aware of the beauty of their heritage. However, as in other villages, mass production crept in and a housing estate was laid out, with the lack of many amenities it should possess. Happily it lies beyond the old boundaries of Puttenham, so it does not detract from the beauty of the village.

If we can trace much of the history of the village by means of its houses, the barns, also, help to fill out the story. Surrey is famous for its barns and Puttenham is well up to the standard of any other village in the county in this respect. The oldest is a large one at Winter's Farm which was built about 1600. From this and others we can appreciate how farming was carried out through the centuries. All the barns follow the accepted pattern. They are weather-boarded and the majority of them have waggon porches. Their size indicates the increasing corn yield and, as a result, the mounting prosperity of the tenant farmers of Puttenham. Thus the houses and barns tell us of the condition in which people lived and died from medieval times to the present day.

The story of Puttenham is not unique. It simply tells of a village conforming to a pattern which appears in almost every rural community in South-east England. The historian or the traditionalist looks back with interest and often with regrets, but no place can remain static; changes are bound to follow each other in ever quickening succession. The concern for the future must now engage all those who live in our villages. How can the best in their past be preserved and passed down to posterity? Only time and a continuing sense of values can answer this question. But let not the village of Puttenham reflect Aldous Huxley's description of it as 'a modest little village nine stories high, with silos, a poultry farm and a small vitamin-D factory'![18]

NOTES

1. Violet Gibbons, 'Puttenham Fifty Years Ago' in 'Papers read at the Puttenham and Wanborough History Society, 1967-1969' (in typescript).
2. Ibid.
3. Ibid.
4. *Surrey Advertiser,* 25 October, 1895.
5. Letters in possession of Puttenham and Wanborough History Society.
6. Sale Particulars issued by 'Messrs. Hewett & Lee for sale by auction at the "White Hart" Hotel, Guildford, on Saturday, Sept. 6th 1902'.
7. Letters in possession of the Puttenham and Wanborough History Society.
8. MS. Minute pasted into the back of the Parish Council Receipt and Payment Book, 1910-1930.
9. Ibid., fol.2.
10. Ibid., fol.6.
11. Ibid., fol.10.
12. *Surrey Advertiser,* 4 August, 1906.
13. See a membership card dated 1 August 1924 and signed by Gilbert Murray, Chairman of the Executive Committee, in the possession of the Puttenham and Wanborough History Society.
14. Documents in possession of the Puttenham and Wanborough History Society.
15. Administration of Estates Act 1925 (15 & 16 Geo.5 c.23).
16. Parish of Puttenham, Vestry Minute Book 1882-1919: Guildford Muniment Room, PSH/PUT/8/27
17. W.G. Hoskins, *History from the Farm,* London 1970, p.16.
18. Aldous Huxley, *Brave New World,* reprinted in Penguin Books, 1955, p.191.

INDEX

PUTTENHAM